The Man Who Invented the Telephone:

ANTONIO

AND THE

ELECTRIC SCREAM

By Sandra Meucci

Branden Books

Boston

Library of Congress Cataloging-in-Publication Data

Meucci, Sandra.
  Antonio and the electric scream : the man who invented
the telephone / by Sandra Meucci.
       p. cm.
  Includes bibliographical references and index.
  ISBN 978-0-8283-2197-6 (pbk. : alk. paper)
1. Meucci, Antonio, 1808-1889--Juvenile literature.
2. Telephone--History--United States--Juvenile literature.
3. Telephone--History--Italy--Juvenile literature.
I. Title.

 TK6018.M4M493 2010
 621.385092--dc22
 [B]

                                         2009053543

Branden Books
PO Box 812094
Wellesley MA 02482

Table of Contents

New York

Cuba

Atlantic Ocean

Italy

Corsica

Africa

Dedication

When I was a child, my grandfather, Giuseppe Meucci, told me that a man named Antonio Meucci first invented the telephone and used it in his New York City home in 1850, when Alexander Graham Bell was still a youth. My grandfather had only a crumpled article to offer in evidence, torn from an Italian newspaper. Because I was taught other-wise and I was unaware of any other articles, documents or books making such a claim, I did not believe my grandfather. Neither did I think about Antonio Meucci, until thirty years later when a friend asked me if I was related to the telephone inventor.

My friend's question stimulated me to learn more about this inventor whose name I bear. Thirty years ago I began researching and compiling information about his life and I have continued until now. Because Antonio was not famous and kept no personal journal, there is little reliable information about his personality or day-to-day life. However, many patents and other legal documents exist as proof of his work and several scholars, particularly Basilio Catania and Giovanni Schiavo, researched official records and chronicled the significant events of his life's journey. I read and consulted these and many other materials to develop this biography of Antonio Meucci and his inventions.

The National Italian American Foundation supported the development of the first manuscript. Dr. Jill Hannum helped with the research and she and Barry Trievel provided editorial assistance to me. The illustrations and cover design were done by Shirley Trievel. I dedicate this book to my grandfather, to my nephews, Alex and Eric Meucci, and to all the children of their generation who I wanted to know about this remarkable scientist.

Introduction

Most readers will be startled at the title of this book, claiming that someone other than the American legend, Alexander Graham Bell, invented the telephone. This book's title, however, is neither a gimmick nor a hoax. There has always been controversy over Bell's claim on the telephone invention. In the 1860s and during the decades that followed, many lawsuits were launched against Bell for having obtained the telephone patent by fraud.

As recently as 2008, a journalist and researcher, Seth Shulman, wrote a book *"Chasing Alexander Graham Bell's Secret: The Telephone Gambit"*, which reveals details of the manner by which Bell obtained the telephone patent. It casts a long shadow of suspicion on Bell's claim to the invention. Shulman, however, knew very little about Antonio Meucci, who was using the telephone *he* invented decades before Bell, or anyone else, applied for that patent.

There have been at least four men to have claimed the priority of the telephone invention. They include Phillip Reis, Elisha Gray, Alexander Graham Bell, and Antonio Meucci. Of these men, Meucci was the first to have a functioning electric telephone which he attempted to patent. In June of 2001 Congressman Vito Fossella introduced a resolution, which was passed in September of 2001 by the United States Congress, recognizing Antonio Meucci for his contribution as the telephone inventor. It reads as follows:

107TH CONGRESS 1ST SESSION
H. RES. 269

Expressing the sense of the House of Representatives to honor the life and achievements of 19th Century Italian-American inventor Antonio Meucci, and his work in the invention of the telephone.

Whereas Antonio Meucci, the great Italian inventor, had a career that was both extraordinary and tragic;

Whereas, upon immigrating to New York, Meucci continued to work with ceaseless vigor on a project he had begun in Havana, Cuba, an invention he later called the telettrofono, involving electronic communications;

Whereas Meucci set up a rudimentary communication link in his Staten Island home that connected the basement with the first floor, and later, when his wife began to suffer from crippling arthritis, he created a permanent link between his lab and his wife's second floor bedroom;

Whereas, having exhausted most of his life's savings in pursuing his work, Meucci was unable to commercialize his invention, though he demonstrated his invention in 1860 and had a description of it published in New York's Italian language newspaper;

Whereas Meucci never learned English well enough to navigate the complex American business community;

Whereas Meucci was unable to raise sufficient funds to pay his way through the patent application process, and thus had to settle for a caveat, a one - year renewable notice of an impending patent, which was first filed on December 28, 1871;

Whereas Meucci later learned that the Western Union affiliate laboratory reportedly lost his working models, and Meucci, who at this point was living on public assistance, was unable to renew the caveat after 1874;

Whereas in March 1876, Alexander Graham Bell, who conducted experiments in the same laboratory where Meucci's materials had been stored, was granted a patent and was thereafter credited with inventing the telephone;

Whereas on January 13, 1887, the Government of the United States moved to annul the patent issued to Bell on the grounds of fraud and misrepresentation, a case that the Supreme Court found viable and remanded for trial;

Whereas Meucci died in October 1889, the Bell patent expired in January 1893, and the case was discontinued as moot without ever reaching the underlying issue of the true inventor of the telephone entitled to the patent; and

Whereas if Meucci had been able to pay the $10 fee to maintain the caveat after 1874, no patent could have been issued to Bell: Now, therefore, be it

Resolved, That it is the sense of the House of Representatives that the life and achievements of Antonio Meucci should be recognized, and his work in the invention of the telephone should be acknowledged

September 25, 2001 (10:41 AM)

This proclamation on its own is not likely to change the way history is written or taught. It was merely a gesture of acknowledgement by a highly legitimate source and, while it is important, it is already obscure. History is a living science – there is always more to be discovered about what we thought we knew as fact. Especially as related to patents, written history often is ignorant of the scientific contribution of people who had limited access to money or connections with influential people. Alexander Graham Bell had all this at his disposal. This book is written as a tribute not only to Meucci's scientific achievements, but also as an acknowledgement that there are others, particularly women and people of color, whose contributions to science have never been marked and whose stories also need to be told.

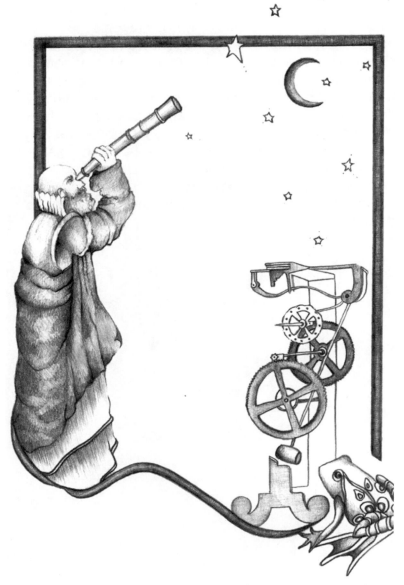

Galileo and Mesmer: the Early Influences, Illustration
by Shirley Trievel

Chapter One

Frogs' Legs and a Curious Boy

I t was the year 1808, and although his family was poor, the infant Antonio Meucci *(May-oo-chee)* was baptized like royalty. All Florentine families took their infants to the Baptistery, the oldest building in the city, to have baptisms performed. Muted light filtered by the gold sculptured "Gates of Paradise" created an artful atmosphere in the baptistery. Michelangelo Buonarroti (1475-1564) named these panels because of their beauty. Centuries before Antonio's birth these ten golden mosaic panels depicted scenes from Bible stories, and were constructed by Lorenzo Ghiberti (1378-1455) to reflect light onto the shining stone interior of the octagonal building. On this day in April the priest immersed the infant in water, and Antonio was baptized or "born again in the life of the spirit."

Antonio's parents, Amatis and Domenica Meucci, held their first-born son as they walked through the streets of Florence until the family arrived back at their home in the neighborhood called San Frediano (*Fred-ee-ah-no*). The Meucci's had only two small rooms in a large house on Via (*Vee ah*) Chiara (*Key-are-ah*), which they shared with three other families. Amatis was an officer of the municipal police, but his salary was not very generous. Antonio's mother, Domenica, helped out with the finances, often working until late at night, knitting cotton or wool socks by the dim light of an oil lamp. Her neighbors bought these socks, knowing how much Domenica needed the extra money.

After Antonio, Domenica gave birth to a little girl, and the Meuccis moved their few pieces of furniture to a larger house. A new child was born every year and a half. There were nine children in all, but four of them died very young. In the nineteenth century, before vaccines and widely available medical care, childhood diseases were a common cause of death. Antonio stayed healthy and showed boundless curiosity about the world around him.

By the time he was in his second year of elementary school his family began thinking that he could accelerate his education. Amatis decided to have his young son attend the Accademia (*ah-kad-ah-me-ah*) as soon as possible. Although Antonio could attend that school free of charge and it was within walking distance, the Accademia was out of reach to a boy so young.

Six years later, in November of 1821, Amatis submitted Antonio's application for admittance to the Accademia. To be admitted, Antonio had to first pass a written test, and it was no doubt the hardest test he had ever taken — for the Accademia was a college. Not long after he delivered his finished exam, a letter arrived at the Meucci home stating that the Florentine Accademia of Fine Art would be delighted to accept Antonio as a pupil. At the age of 13, he would be its youngest student.

Because his classes were held in a convent at San Caterina near the *Piazza* [pee-ah-tsa] San Marco in Florence, the building gave the appearance of a nunnery. Mr. Gori, the headmaster, greeted the new student and led him on a tour of the entire campus.

Antonio, who had never been to a college before, followed Mr. Gori's lead to the Museum of the Machines, where Galileo's pendulum clock was on display. Two hundred years earlier Galileo Galilei (1564–1642) was old and almost blind when he developed the clock. Early in Galileo's life, he noticed that time could be measured by the swing of a pendulum, which took the same time to make a long swing as it did to make a short one. The invention of the pendulum clock came at a favorable time. After the Renaissance, there were urgent commercial pressures to find a way to measure time more accurately so that navigation at sea could be improved.

After visiting the Museums of Physics and Natural History they proceeded on to the Museum of Music. Antonio's studies eventually brought him into all of the many buildings that made up the entire campus of the school. The school reflected a holistic view of human culture, science and art taught side-by-side. Most of the graduates were awarded the title "engineer," an esteemed title for it implied that the bearer was from a socially distinguished family. The students specialized in applied sciences, and their attendance in class was quite free and informal.

Beginning with the basics all first-year students at the Accademia took the same classes — the elements of drawing and perspective, anatomy, and art history. After the first year, they would be free to study painting, sculpture, piano, violin, mathematics, and chemistry and he took a keen interest in chemistry.

> **Galileo**, an Italian physicist and astronomer, is best known today for his pioneering development of the telescope which, when he began, was about as powerful as modern binoculars. He worked with lens polishers of Venice to obtain the strongest possible lenses. Using his improved and more powerful lenses in his later telescope, he identified the four largest satellites of Jupiter, mountains and craters on the moon, and he discovered that the Milky Way is composed of stars. With the sophisticated telescope he built it was possible to view objects at a magnification of twenty times. After much "stargazing," Galileo found solid evidence to support the theory that the earth revolves around the sun and is *not* the center of the universe, as was believed in his time. Galileo's discovery confirmed the findings, about the earth's relation to the sun, by an earlier astronomer, Nicolaus Copernicus (1473–1543).

Antonio's male colleagues were much older. In 1821 no Italian colleges or universities accepted female students. (Five years after he finished his program of studies, however, the first young women were admitted.) His classmates were mostly from "well-to-do" families, and this, too, widened the gap between them and the new boy.

Following his teachers' directions he read classic scientific works, books on Galileo and Leonardo da Vinci (1452-1514). Antonio entered college at a time before major break-throughs in electrical science had occurred, before the discovery of the light bulb, telephone, or automobile. In the 1820's scientists in France (Andre Ampere) and England (Michael Faraday and William Surgeon) were occupied by the study of the effects of magnetic fields on electrical currents, important principles underlying the development of generators and motors. Although batteries were in use then, they were not yet able to produce a constant electrical current, so the application of battery technology was limited. Academically Antonio was focused on drawing, chemistry, and mechanics, in which he displayed remarkable constructive talent in his first two years of intensive studies.

During this time, he learned that in 1609 Galileo had begun building and using rudimentary telescopes, placing mirrors and glass inside long tubular chambers. Looking through the chamber by moonlight, Galileo examined the sky and located the position of the moon and planets.

Leonardo da Vinci, a scientist who lived a century before Galileo, was considered to be one of the greatest masters of Italy's High Renaissance. Best known today as a painter, he brought his great skill as an artist to his scientific diagrams, drawing beautiful models of such fantastic ideas as flying machines with bird-like wings to catch the wind. No flying machines actually existed in da Vinci's time, and the Wright brothers would not fly the first airplane until four hundred years later in 1903, but the great artist da Vinci was diagramming what he thought were scientific possibilities. Among his prophetic inventions were an underwater diving suit, a parachute, and three different types of aircraft. He formulated valid theories about how continents are formed and calculated the effects of the moon on the tides. Not long after reading about da Vinci's inventions, Antonio, too, began to draw detailed diagrams.

His imagination was sparked by the story of Luigi Galvani *(Loo-ee-gee Gal-vohn-ee)* (1737-1798), an Italian biologist who claimed to have discovered electricity inside the bodies of animals. Galvani experimented on frogs, which he dissected and placed on a metal sheet. Whenever he touched one of the dissected frog's nerves with his steel scalpel, a leg would twitch. At the time of his studies at the Accademia, in the 1820s, different theories explained the origin and nature of electricity. Because Galvani found that the frog's legs twitched whenever he brought them into contact with two different metals (he usually used brass and iron), he concluded that the leg muscles were producing "animal electricity."

Galvani sent a report of his findings to an Italian physicist, his friend Alessandro Volta (1745-1827). Volta repeated the experiments and decided that Galvani had drawn the wrong conclusion. There was no animal electricity. Volta suggested that the frog's leg twitched not because of electricity inside the muscle but because a *chemical reaction* took place when brass and iron came in contact with each other and with the fluids in the frog's body. Galvani was furious at being contradicted, and a bitter fight broke out between the two men.

Volta continued to experiment and soon tried an approach that did not involve animal tissue at all. He sandwiched a piece of paper that had been soaked in salt water (which he thought would play the same role as the fluid in the frog's leg) between a piece of silver and a piece of zinc. When he connected wires to the metals, he found that an electrical current flowed. At last, there was experimental proof of why the frog's leg twitched — it was the result of the electrical charge created when the metals and fluids came into contact with one another. This scientific fact was going to play a major role in Antonio's future and pointed the direction for his own discoveries.

Fireworks over the River Arno, Illustration by Shirley Trievel

Chapter Two

The Fireworks Go "Off"

A ntonio carefully studied the work of Alessandro Volta. Volta developed a series of purely mechanical devices, which he used to generate and conduct electrical currents. No frogs were involved. His arrangement of metal disks separated by paper disks soaked in acid and salt was the first battery. Volta constructed the battery so that he could increase or decrease the intensity of the electrical current, depending on how many disks he inserted. The fluid,

> In 1829 A.C. Becquerel studied the passage of the current in Volta's battery and noted that the current created hydrogen ions, which caused a rapid drop in electromotive force. The hydrogen ions clustered around the battery's positive pole. He then introduced substances capable of reacting with the hydrogen (to form water for example) and maintained the continuous electrical flow of the current.

acid, and salt mixture acted as a conductor, promoting a chemical reaction between metals that resulted in a stream of electric current.

With materials available to him at the Accademia, Antonio was able to construct his own simple batteries, by piling zinc and silver discs and using one wire to connect the zinc disc on the bottom to a wire from the silver one on top. Though repeated electrical sparks were produced whenever the wires touched, this simple battery did not maintain a continuous current of electricity. There was a serious shortcoming in the Volta battery, but no explanation was offered until later that decade.

Antonio became steeped in the art of battery technology in the 1820s. As he proceeded with such satisfying studies, he learned there was financial trouble at home. Amatis Meucci was forced to ask Antonio to find paying work, because the family needed income. His sisters helped however they could. Adelaide, who had just turned twelve, earned a little money doing small embroidery works. Ten-year-old Luisa worked alongside her mother around the house. The other children were still too young to be of any help.

Amatis was able to find Antonio a job with the Buon Governo (the governor). Near the world-famous Uffizi (*Oo-feet-zee*)art gallery in central Florence, there was a jungle of government offices where passports were stamped and taxes were collected. Amatis had a desk in the lobby of the main office, in the Piazza del Gran Duca, and his title was Custodian of the President. Antonio, who had just turned sixteen, didn't have a fancy title. He was just an entry-level guard assigned to the Porta San Niccolo (St. Nicholas Gate), the left bank of the Arno (river that runs through Florence).

Men and boys in uniform were stationed at Florence's borders. Now, Antonio was one of them. Like the other guards, he was assigned to work an eight-hour "shift." His job was to stop all the coaches and carriages coming into the city, inspect the drivers' goods and permits. and collect taxes from them. To help secure the city from intruders, two large cannons were situated on the top of a hill near the gate. Early every morning Antonio wrapped himself in his new uniform. He performed his duties so well and with such courtesy that he was often asked to work two shifts in a row, sixteen hours at a stretch. He was promoted to Assistant Gatekeeper. When his work shifts allowed, Antonio went to the Accademia.

His duties became more complex after the promotion, and Antonio soon joined the team of guards assigned to light the fireworks whenever there was a major celebration. On one such occasion, the people of Florence were celebrating the birth of a child to the Grand Duchess, who was married to the Grand Duchy, Leopold II, who was considered the Buon Governo (Governor) of Tuscany at this time.

The plan for the celebration

> At this time, the Austrian empire ruled Tuscany – the region of Italy that includes Florence. Its form of government was a monarchy, and royal families inherited the power to govern. The Grand Duchess, Maria Carolina of Saxony, was part of one such royal family, which held powers similar to those of a governor.

was to light up the town square, the Piazza del Granduca, with fire-works for three nights in a row, and Antonio was put in charge of launching them. The launchers were set up across the Arno River from the piazza town square. Each launcher held a cylinder containing eight to ten rockets, and each rocket was designed to produce an impressive variety of colors, forms and sounds.

The fireworks were under the direction of a forty-six year-old umbrella maker and fireman named Gaetano Baratti (*Guy-tawn-oh Ba-raw-tea*). Antonio's education in chemistry gave him an advantage in understanding the role of the various chemicals being used. Like all the Italian firework makers of his time, Baratti used chlorates instead of nitrates (which had dominated in the past), because chlorates created more explosive oxidizers. Firework makers were all trying to get more intense colors by heating chlorates – metal salts such as calcium chloride or sodium chloride.

Baratti inserted the salts into dough-like lumps called "stars" that were just a few centimeters in diameter. When ignited these stars would produce both sound and light effects. Antonio knew enough chemistry to realize that Baratti's mixture of strontium, lithium salts and lithium carbonate would produce a red flame and that the combination of sodium salts and sodium chloride would produce yellow. When Baratti carefully packed the stars into cardboard compartments within the firework shell, he was satisfied that he was going to give Antonio the best possible rockets to launch.

The first two nights everything went perfectly. Antonio and his crew climbed the scaffold that had been constructed especially for setting off fireworks and, after igniting the main fuse, the rockets blazed across the River Arno. Once launched, a wick inside each rocket burned upward toward the cardboard compartments containing the stars. When the wick reached the compartments, the highly explosive components ignited to produce the desired effect—a loud explosion and a bright flash of colors. Thousands of people witnessed the show in the sky.

On the third night, when Antonio lit the fuse, the rockets again soared over the River Arno, even higher than before. But they didn't turn downward into the water as planned. They kept right on going, all the way across the river into the crowd gathered on the other side. Sparks rained down like thunderbolts in every direction, singeing spectators in the piazza.

Across the Arno from where Antonio stood, sirens wailed, stopping the whole celebration. Police reports of the incident document that alarmed, agitated spectators retreated from their balconies to peer out from behind their windows at the commotion in the streets surrounding the piazza. The spectators acted completely bewildered as to what had gone wrong.

The police were soon on the scene. On Antonio's side of the river, they went straight for the gatekeepers who had been setting off the rockets. They easily found Antonio and his two crew members, Franci and Andreini. The young men were perched near the rocket launchers, and the officers arrested all three and took them downtown, where they were presented with the results of a hurried investigation of the incident. The sparks from the fireworks had ignited a young girl's dress, and a rocket had fallen upon a man, burning his hair. This man reported having been stunned by the event. In all, eight people were injured though none seriously so. The costs of the damages were estimated, including the price of a silk scarf and a dress as well as medical bills for treating three men whose faces had been burned. When everything was tallied, the final sum was 100 lire (equivalent to 885,000 lire or $737 in 1990).

According to the records of the investigation in 1825, "...*each of the three defendants directly took part in lighting the Rockets of the Funnels, which caused the inconveniences mentioned. All ten of these Funnels were lighted by them alone.*" Included with the documents was a signed statement from a boy, whose identity was not made clear, but who testified that he had heard Antonio brag that, "**Something special is in store.**" The investigation concluded that all three of the gatekeepers had been responsible for the errant rocket, but the officers suspected that Antonio had been the main culprit.

After the incident with the rockets, policemen routinely followed Antonio. The authorities suspected that he was involved with a group of political protesters who were trying to overthrow the government of Florence at that time.Though Antonio was likely aware of the people who were protesting Austria's control of much of Italy, there is no evidence that he was a member of their group. Called the Carboneria (*carb-oh-nair-ee-ah*), this secret society made up of educated Italians often clashed with the local government, though not violently so. However, the people of Florence took sides during these clashes, leading to riots and rebellions. Because Antonio was deemed responsible for the misguided fireworks, the police suspected that he might be using his position as Assistant Gatekeeper to incite the Carboneria to spark more flames.

A short time after the fireworks accident, a policeman tapped Antonio on the shoulder and took him to the police station. There, the Chief Gatekeeper quickly confronted Antonio with his "crime" of neglecting to nail down a wooden platform. The platform covered a huge pit in the ground, and the Chief wrote in his statement: "*The deeds on the whole reveal that Meucci is a careless young man, who tends to associate with the soldiers rather than to attend tirelessly to his Duty.*"

Antonio admitted that he *did* forget to cover the pit, as his supervisor had told him to do. Once again, someone had been hurt. A fellow named Luigi Ficini, another of the Assistant Gatekeepers, had fallen into the pit and broken his leg.

Antonio was presented with yet another written complaint, this time from the Superintendent of San Spirito, whose jurisdiction covered the area of Antonio's job post. He called for a full investigation of "*this Meucci, who neglected to warn his fellow gatekeeper about the pit, which was being used as a toilet, when this fellow found himself knee high in it!*" The complaint concludes, "*I therefore believe that this defendant deserves to be mortified by five days in prison, for I deem such a measure opportune in order for him to become more cautious in his behavior in all circumstances.*"

The Buon Governo (Governor) heard about the incident very quickly and imposed an even harsher penalty. The Buon Governo wrote: *"Meucci shall be sentenced to eight days in prison, three on bread and water, and he will have to pay for the expenses of the deeds and for the damages caused to the offended party."*

That same evening at 5 PM, Amatis Meucci escorted his son to the police Superintendent to begin his sentence. The Police Superintendent, a man named Callepi, knew and liked Amatis, and he encouraged Amatis to write a letter of appeal to the Buon Governo. That evening Amatis wrote his plea to the Buon Governo. He took it to Callepi the next morning. After rewording appropriately by Callepi it stated:

*"**Memorandum***
To the Most Illustrious Sir Knight President of the Buon Governo

The Son of the undersigned who is in Prison has not committed crimes such as to taint the honor of his Family, nor is he Guilty of any other offense if not lack of consideration and carelessness to be attributed to his youth, and which did not allow him to reflect on the damages which he has involuntarily caused; Such circumstances torment the Heart of a Father, who Humbly Implores The Goodness, The Clemency and The Mercy of your Most Illustrious Excellency, to ascribe to his Youth and lack of experience what the Son is Guilty of…
And therefore Begs you to be so kind as to reduce the right Punishment to comfort an Afflicted Mother and to Forgive him the invol-

*untary rather than deliberate shortcomings
and to condescend to allow him to return to
his duty as Gatekeeper, the Suspension of
which increases day after day the new trou-
bles that fall upon this Innocent and Unfortu-
nate Family."*

Forwarding Amitas's plea to the Buon Governo, Callepi added a letter of his own as an introduction, that
contained the following passage:

*"...as can be deduced also from the state-
ments of the witnesses heard, who spoke of
him as a careless and absent-minded
youth...it is my opinion that, accepting the petition forwarded by his father, the sentence of
detention pronounced for his son should be
reduced by three days.*

*And with all due respect and regard it is
with honor that I place myself at the service of
your Most Illustrious Excellency.*

*From the S. Spirito Precinct, 9 June 1825,
Most devout and obliged*

D. Callepi, Police Superintendent"

Callepi also looked favorably on Antonio, and saw to it
that he ate well on the night before the prescribed
three days of water and bread. As Antonio ate his last
full meal for days, served with coarse bread on a
modest wooden table, he conversed with his fellow
prisoner. His father petitioned for his release, and
Amatis' plea was forwarded to the Buon Governo. A
reply arrived promptly. It said that the Governo was

31

" . . . accepting the petition forwarded by his father, the sentence of detention pronounced for his son should be reduced by three days."

Antonio would have to endure five days, three on bread and water, in what must have seemed like a dungeon.

Italian Opera Singer, Illustration by Shirley Trievel

Chapter Three

The Opera Singer and the Dressmaker

After his release from jail, Antonio resumed his post at the Porta San Niccolo, but his superiors and comrades made such trouble for him that he was forced to leave in July of 1830. Twenty-two-year old Antonio searched throughout Florence in his quest to find another job. Undeterred by work and a short jail sentence he managed to finish his studies at the Accadamia two years earlier in 1828, completing his degree in the school of chemistry and mechanics, and he was ready to begin his occupation. He found his way to the opera theater and began a life that would forever more be filled with the sound of singing.

In 1833 when Antonio was 25 years old, his acquaintance, Dante Margheri (*Don-tay Mar-gair-ee*), who was the custodian of the Teatro della Pergola, advised Antonio to speak with the theater's manager, Alessandro Lanari (*Al-ey-son-droh La-nare-ey*). The theater was a majestic building, which cost what would today be equivalent of billions to build and was then financed by the famous Florentine Medici family. While it was soundproofed against the noises of coaches and carriages on the street, it was also insulated from the smell of the horses drawing those carriages. Looking into the hall, one could see rows of seats, some of them very high and very far away from the stage. The interior of the 900-seat room was quite dark, for only candles lighted it. Gas lighting was introduced years later, in 1837. The theater, like a cavern, needed brightening so everyone could see the stage.

Looking for someone in charge, he located the Chief Stagehand, Artemio Canovetti (*Are-teem-ee-oh Can-oh-vet-tee*), whose job it was to set up pulleys and counterweights for moving the scenery. Antonio mentioned to the gentleman that he already had some relevant experience. This had been at the Quarconia (*kwar-cone-ee-ah*) Theater, also in Florence, where he had occasionally been hired to produce special effects such as lightning, thunder, rain, wind, and so on. Every theater had its own system of producing special effects, such as sheets of glass with one side colored blue placed in front of the candles that lit the scenes to simulate the effect of daytime. But the Teatro della Pergola featured effects that were among the most spectacular in all the theaters.

Knowing that the Pergola was *always* in need of people with such talents, the Chief Stagehand directed him to go see the Pergola's owner, the great impresario Allessandro Lanari. He wasted no time and hired Antonio as a technician.

Lanari introduced Antonio to the crew as **Signore [Mr.]** Meucci. As he gave the new employee a whirlwind tour, he showed Meucci where he would have a workshop and lodging, and quickly discussed the question of salary. This was a fortunate professional opportunity for Antonio, one that allowed him to address problems of optics, mechanics, chemistry, electricity and physics in the performing arts, in an establishment frequented by thousands of people.

All Antonio's hard work at the Accademia had finally paid off. In a lightning move, he was put in charge of lighting and sound at one of the leading theatrical establishments in all of Italy. The Pergola had been built with the latest technology (for the year 1833), so Antonio could apply his skills in chemistry, electricity and mechanics. His first step was to make improvements in the lighting. He set up a laboratory in his tiny workroom behind the stage. Remembering that Galileo had used hundreds of finely cut mirrors inside his telescope to make it possible for him to see the planets in the sky at night, Antonio repositioned the mirrors that were already behind each candle so that they would magnify the light in all directions. He also worked with a newly purchased electrostatic machine, which produced artificial lightning by generating strong electrical charges. The theater's patrons benefited from the improved technical effects during the performances.

Having solved the lighting problems, Antonio turned to the matter of the theater's poor acoustics. Though they could now see the singers, the patrons at the back of the theater could barely hear them. Antonio began working on a megaphone-like device with a metallic component that would amplify and direct the sound of the performers' voices. Fortunately or unfortunately, Lanari refused to let it be used during performance because it was so unattractive. The stagehands, however, immediately saw a good use for the megaphones. The audience always grew impatient during the relatively long time it took to change the stage sets between scenes. The time was cut by half when the stagehands began using the megaphones to communicate with one another across the large theater when changing sets.

His work at the theater occurred during the times of the rehearsals and he lodged there during the times when performances occurred. His room was situated away from the rest of the theater and was accessible only by a small wooden ladder that led to a platform from which a long and broad spiral staircase climbed to the building's high ceiling. At the very top was a small room with a window that overlooked an interior courtyard. This was Antonio's laboratory. It looks much the same today, after one hundred and seventy years. It had a little iron door that had been painted red, and though very quaint, it beaconed few visitors.

During the course of his three years at this theater Antonio met two people who were to become life-long companions. The first was Lorenzo Salvi, a famous tenor who sang occasionally at the Opera della Pergo. (A tenor has the highest male voice in operatic performances.) The second was Esterre Mochi (*Esstir Mow-chee*), the theater's dressmaker and the young woman who was to become his wife.

Esterre was two and a half years younger than Antonio and she shared many similarities with him. Her family, for instance, moved from apartment to apartment continually, because of their financial situation. Esterre, too, began her profession at a young age. When she was ten years old, she worked work as an apprentice for a local tailor. After five years, at the age of 15, she mastered her trade and was hired by the Teatro della Pergola.

Their courtship was brief and soon a marriage proposal was offered. Antonio was 26 years old when he married Esterre Mochi in the grand Saint Maria Novella Church in Florence, Esther's family church. Thus, the young couple began their life and travels together.

At that time, Italian opera was fast becoming famous around the world, and soon after Antonio met Esterre and Lorenzo, Lanari decided to move the entire opera company. He intended to cross the Atlantic Ocean to Cuba to help establish a new opera theater there. Havana, Cuba was a cultural center for the new Americas and Italian opera was considered one of the finest cultural forms.

At the new Cuban theater, both Antonio's and Esterre's positions, responsibilities and salaries would increase. It seemed at the time that they would be gone from Florence for only five years, the term of the contract with the Cuban impresario. They had the additional good fortune of traveling to Havana with their new friend, Lorenzo Salvi, who also agreed to help establish Italian opera in Cuba.

Rehabilitated Pirate Ship—Coccodrillo, Illustration by
Shirley Trievel

Chapter Four

Coccodrillo Sails to Havana

Young Antonio, with his new bride by his side, stepped into a carriage pulled by two thick-bodied horses. They were leaving Florence, the only home either of them had ever known. Traveling this night in October of 1835 through the Italian countryside their horses clopped along dirt roads until late into the dark night. The horses couldn't pull the carriage for more than a few hours at a time without getting tired, so new horses were harnessed to the carriage at each of three stops.

The journey took them to the Port of Livorno, on the Ligurian Sea, which opens onto the Mediterranean Sea, where they were to meet the ship that would sail them to Havana, Cuba.

Approaching the port, all they could see was a huge sail that appeared to float above the water, but as the carriage drew closer two hardy masts and a hull appeared. Because their previous travels were limited it is doubtful they had ever before seen anything quite like this ship *Coccodrillo,* [Ko-ko-dree-o]. Captain Lombardo later told Antonio that *Coccodrillo,* which means crocodile, had once been a pirate ship, and everyone was well aware that there were still plenty of pirates sailing other ships on the Atlantic Ocean. In fact, the ship was equipped with cannons on each side in order to defend it from any pirates who still may be lying in wait.

The pirates had relinquished the *Coccodrillo*, and now it transported cargo and passengers on trans-Atlantic voyages. Immediately before its commission with the Italian Opera Company, the ship had solely been used to transport cargo. It was renovated for this trip with cabins added. Using this ship was somewhat of a disguise, designed to hide the fact that *Coccodrillo* was transporting passengers, Antonio included, who were being followed by the Italian government (which was then the office of then the Grand Duchey of Tuscany). Because Antonio and several of the other passengers were associated with the efforts to unify the Italian nation, against the will of the existing Grand Duchey, they would have been apprehended upon boarding a more ordinary passenger vessel. But the Grand Duchey's soldiers did not suspect, nor did they check the passenger list of the *Coccodrillo*, for rebels.

Planks were laid down from the ship's deck to the wharf so the passengers could board. Though it was 3:30 in the morning, many relatives stood on the dock to wish their loved ones bon voyage! It was customary for the relatives to bring freshly baked bread and cheeses wrapped in straw for their friends and relatives to take along on the voyage. Many tearful good-byes were said at such departures as Cuba was very far away and it was never certain if passengers would, in fact, return. Antonio said his own good-byes just the night before. His father, Amatis, then believed that Antonio would only stay in Cuba for a few years – just long enough to get away from the bad luck he had had in Italy – and then he would return home to his family. But Amatis was never to see his eldest son again.

The ship's cargo included an estimated 35 tons of props and equipment necessary to set up the opera stage in Havana. The ship was designed to hold up to 275 tons and the rest of the usable space was converted into cabins in the passenger section, which had bunk–beds. There were also a dozen or so luxury cabins with large, comfortable beds, and those had been assigned to the dignitaries within the opera company. Antonio and Esterre were graced with good accommodations, and the trip for them was a honeymoon. Their friend Lorenzo Salvi had a nearby cabin, and the Meucci's fell asleep each night to the sound of the waves and occasionally to operatic singing. Antonio's life seemed finally to be "on course," with his best friend and his wife by his side and all of them sailing into a promising future.

Departing on October 5, 1835, eighty-one passengers lived together on the *Coccodrillo* for two and a half months and they became like a family, with all its kindnesses and squabbles. The ship was as slow as a basking crocodile as it moved through the water, for it relied only on its sails and lacked the benefit of a steam engine. Ships with steam engines were faster, but they were far more dangerous, as the steam engines often blew up (See Chapter 9). They were relatively new, as the first steam engine trans-Atlantic crossing occurred only seven years before the Meucci's departure. Crossing the Atlantic without the benefit of a steam engine, still took the *Coccodrillo* only half the time it took Christopher Columbus to cross the Atlantic.

Coccodrillo took 72 days to reach Havana on December 16, 1835. The Captain carefully selected a route that was defended by the naval Spanish Armada. After one day of navigation they reached the northern Coast of Corsica, where the passengers could observe the island's lush vegetation. This island, owned by France, is suspended between the Ligurian and Mediterranean Seas. Sailing then for five days on the open sea toward Spain, they sighted the small island of Menorca, the first of the Balearic Islands in the Mediterranean Sea. Then heading Southwest, *Coccodrillo's* Captain Lombardo reached the Straight of Gibralter, that narrow passage separating the Mediterranean Sea from the Atlantic Ocean, which bordered Spain to the north and Morocco to the south. From the Balearic Islands *Coccodrillo* took a week to reach the end of the Mediterranean Sea.

After another week and a half, the ship moored at Gomera, in the Canary Islands. This journey followed the route taken by Christopher Columbus heading for Central and South America. The Canary Islands were and still are owned by the Spanish. Here the ship was graced by the favorable thrust of the trade winds, which blow constantly from northeast to southwest, giving a tremendous boost to sailing vessels on trans-Atlantic voyages. As the days passed on the *Coccodrillo*, Antonio used the time to organize his notebooks from school, and Esterre kept busy sewing. As soon as the ship passed out of the Mediterranean Sea and through the Gibraltar Strait into the Atlantic Ocean however, their shipmate Bertu grew worried.

Coccodrillo still bore its original sails from its days as a pirate ship, and now was sailing at a frisky six and a half knots (the unit of measure for ship's speed). Though the sails had been repaired many times, they should long since have been replaced. Because they were moving at such high speed, Bertu wondered how much pressure from the trade wind the sails would bear before shredding. A crowd soon gathered around Bertu, whose worried checking of the sails had attracted attention. Soon, however, the hefty winds ceased and calm was restored. *Coccodrillo* had sailed over one hundred miles that day, moving at more than six knots.

Still, the ship was vulnerable to storms and predicting weather is always a tricky business, but knowing the changes in humidity (how much moisture is in the air) helps. The captain had no way to determine how the humidity was changing, and if humidity was on the rise, it often predicted storms ahead. Even if the captain thought that the humidity was increasing, he couldn't know for certain if the *Coccodrillo* was about to encounter a big storm. What he needed was a gauge that would

By the late nineteenth century a variety of instruments had been devised to measure atmospheric humidity (the amount of water vapor in the air). Some absorbed and weighed water vapor – Leonardo da Vinci earlier used a ball of wool that became moister and heavier as the relative humidity rose. Others absorbed the moisture chemically and measured the change in vapor tension. Still other techniques included cooling the air to the temperature where condensation begins (dew point) then measured the relative dew points.

show changes in the air's moisture level as they occurred.

 Antonio pondered the problem while on this voyage
and consulted his studies and books, which kept him
busy for much of the trip. Antonio began experimenting with many substances available on the ship, ex-
posing them to air and noting the different quantities
of moisture in them. Whalebone acted well for his
purposes. He shaved a long, thin piece of whalebone,
coiled it into a helix, varnished the outer layer of the
coil of bone, positioned an index within it, and devised
a shipboard instrument to accurately measure the
relative humidity in the air. Much later in his life, Antonio patented his improvement in hygro-meters.

One can learn a great deal about ships and sailing on
a passenger vessel traveling between the old and
new worlds. Curious passengers on the *Coccodrillo*
observed the shipmate holding a long rope, the end of
which trailed off the side of the ship. The boy, Bertu,
was measuring the ship's speed. Bertu had tied a long
coil of rope to a log and thrown the log into the sea.
The rope had been prepared earlier with a series of
knots in it, one every sixteen yards. While holding the
rope with one hand as the coil unwound like a snake
from the deck, he held an hourglass in the other hand,
a device he used to determine how much time
passed. The log tended to remain relatively stationary
as the ship moved away from it, and the coils of rope
were slowly pulled into the sea. Bertu counted the
number of knots that passed through his fingers, and
that's how the speed of a ship was measured. *Coccodrillo* normally sailed at three knots, and when there
were high winds, as fast as 7 knots. A knot is just over
one mile an hour.

After two and a half months at sea, the ship reached the shores of Havana, Cuba, and a new chapter in Antonio's life was about to begin. He left his boyhood behind and was about to take his place as a man in the New World.

Gas Lights of Havana, Illustration by Shirley Trievel

Chapter Five

Water, Buckles and Swords

Havana welcomed the *Coccodrillo* to its shores on December 16, 1835. People lined up at the Canal del Puerto (*Poo-air-toe*) to watch the opera company disembark. Setting their feet on solid shore after several months at sea, Antonio, Esterre and Lorenzo caught their first glimpse of the Cuban capital's low stone houses and many towering churches. Horse and ox-drawn carts were waiting at the port to transport the entire opera company and their bags to their lodgings.

As the animals pulled the carts along the streets of Havana, Antonio and Esterre got a full view of the city that was to be their home for the next fifteen years. Immediately apparent was that the glass in the gas lamps that lined every city street was designed to disperse the light in all directions. This made them seem to burn especially brightly. Like those gas lamps, Antonio's years in Cuba were to be the brightest of his life.

The opera company drew plenty of attention as it trundled along in the carriages, called "volantas." The volantas had huge wheels that rose well above the occupants' heads and they were designed for travel on bumpy roads. The name means "flying carriage" and the voltana delivered Antonio and Esterre to the guest house where they were to stay. Lorenzo did not lodge with them. He was by then one of the most famous Italian tenors in the world, and was driven on to one of Havana's palaces.

African slaves greeted the Meuccis on the evening of their arrival and delivered an invitation to attend dinner the following evening with Don Francisco Marty, the Impresario of the Tacon Opera Theater named after the governor Don Miguel Tacon Y Rosique. Antonio and Esterre soon learned that slavery was a fact of life in the new Americas, and both Cuba and the United States were major traders in slaves from Africa. First brought to Cuba by Spaniards in 1511, African slaves began a permanent settlement there. There were also Chinese semi-slaves, for in 1847 six hundred Chinese arrived in Cuba, contracted to work for eight years at a mere $4 per month for Spanish colonialists. By the time the Meuccis reached Havana, slaves were working not only as domestic laborers, but they also provided the labor for the Cuban sugar plantations. The sugar industry was a big part of the Cuban economy. At the time Antonio and Estherre lived in Cuba, African slaves made up nearly half (45%) of the entire Cuban population. Slavery was not abolished in Cuba until much later in 1886, as a result of many slave uprisings, which occurred while the Meuccis were in Havana.

As the Meuccis took their positions with the Tacon Opera Theater, the first order of business was to get the company's new theater built. The owner unfolded a huge sheaf of blueprints and asked Antonio to work on the design. Antonio was confronted with the plans that seemed to be for a coliseum, not for a theater. The proposed building was far too large for proper acoustics, so Antonio thought of ways to overcome the negative effects of the architectural design on the sound. He was aware that the character of the *space in which sound was produced* affected the clarity and audibility of the sound. This was the fundamental principle of acoustics in the era before sound could be amplified electronically, and before mathematics was applied to acoustical engineering.

In the late eighteenth and early nineteenth centuries, many scientists theorized about the way sound waves travel through the air, through water or any other medium. They relied almost entirely on observation of how sound travels and how it is modified in the course of that travel. Because the quality of sound was so important to a good operatic performance, Antonio's observations were critical. He devised a way to incorporate a flow of water into the overall *resonance chamber* of the theater. A resonance chamber is essentially any surrounding medium within which sound waves vibrate. Antonio's work on this occurred fifteen years before the American inventor Joseph Henry (1851) identified the role of room volume, shape and surface absorption on the behavior of sound waves.

Antonio knew also that the quality of the music depended on the paths by which sound traveled to the listener, how far it traveled, how powerful its original source was, and the nature of the barriers between the source and listener. In the particular case of this new opera building, the size and volume of the theater caused problems with the low frequency tones. The reflection of the sound waves between the theater floor and ceiling, or "standing wave pattern" of low tones, resulted in the generation of loud, and highly undesirable sound because the wave pattern created by low frequency tones matched the frequency tones of the theater itself. This wave pattern could be altered in a variety of ways, and since he could not change the size of the theater, he instead changed its volume. Antonio rerouted parts of a nearby river to flow through the theater's basement. The sheet of water that formed in the basement became part of a resonance chamber, which reduced the volume of the theater. By November 1837 the building was finished, and the Gran Teatro de Tacon Theater opened its doors for its first opera performance.

Over the following year Antonio had set up his laboratory and Esterre had established her tailoring workshop at the Tacon Theater, which faced a large plaza that was always in a bustle of activity. For the next 15 years they lived in a four-room apartment adjacent to the opera house, and they often toured the Plaza at night after work. The entire square was a public market where merchants and traders displayed their goods and farmers sold fruit and vegetables from atop overturned wooden boxes.

The abundance of food in Havana and the way the Cubans around him indulged in wine and cigars stood in sharp contrast with the hardships endured by Antonio's own family in Florence. The pace of life in Cuba was familiar to Antonio, though much like his life in Italy. As noted by an historian of life in Havana in the 1840s:

"*People got up early in Havana, at six o'clock in the morning there are already many traders at the docks, breathing fresh sea air and trying to catch up with the latest news. At seven o'clock everything started moving: cranes containing sugar, sacks of coffee and tobacco. All goods are transported by donkeys, horses or mules. The carts make such a deafening noise. Everyone works until three o'clock in the afternoon and then returns home for lunch. They love to enjoy life. Once the working day is over, Spaniards want to relax, strolling around, seeing people, listening to music.*"

Though they were busy during the day with work at the theater, the Meuccis' evenings were free, and their many Cuban friends often visited them. One evening, the visitor was Don Manuel Pastor (*Mahn-well Pahstore*), who wanted Antonio's ideas about how to improve the poor quality of Havana's water. Antonio was familiar with waterworks, for his home city of Florence had an elaborate system of canals and aqueducts, all of them equipped with chemical filters to eliminate foreign bodies and impurities.

Pastor supervised Havana's entire water system, and though he was a competent civil engineer, he had no means by which to determine the actual properties of the water. A simple examination revealed that the water used for washing clothes left the clothes discolored. A glass of Havana's water had sediment at the bottom. Dishes washed in the water had spots. Antonio analyzed the total mineral content of the water isolating the positive ions, which contained calcium, magnesium and sodium. These minerals should have been compensated by other negative ions of bicarbonate, sulfate and chloride. Antonio discovered that Havana's water was 'hard,' full of calcium and magnesium chlorides and sulfates, which could not be eliminated simply by boiling. The crusty deposits of these chemicals damaged the water pipes and made the water taste terrible, unsuitable even for washing because no suds would form. The problem was so extreme that most people purchased spring water from merchants who had it transported to Havana in huge jugs. African slaves carried the jugs on their heads from house to house and delivered the water throughout the entire city of Havana.

Antonio made a thorough examination of the water filters throughout the entire city and his conclusion was that they were no good. He knew that he needed to chemically neutralize the corrosive effects of the calcium and magnesium, or 'soften' the water, but his efforts to do so were not successful until after he gave up on the old filters and developed new ones. He treated the new filters chemically by applying lime and sodium, and Antonio installed them in the aqueduct leading to the underground water pipes. This softened the water so well that it could again be used for drinking and bathing. Don Manuel had the new filtering system, Antonio's first successful invention in Havana, installed throughout the entire city.

Esterre, too, met with success in Havana. She kept busy creating and sewing all the costumes for the opera singers. Sewing machines were not available until 1850, fifteen years after the Meuccis arrived in Havana so Esterre sewed everything by hand. Each opera had approximately ten performers, and, of course, each opera had to have a separate set of costumes.

Because their costumes had to be "fitted" at her workshop at least twice for every performance, Esterre got to know all of the singers intimately. She commanded each performer to stand still as they stood perched on a stool in front of her, often with a half-sewn garment hanging on them. Esterre's practice was to take a first measurement of the length of a singer's legs, arms and torso before beginning to sew and then another measurement after the costume was made. This second measurement let her know where to take the fabric in or let it out so the garment would fit just right.

Paying attention to every detail of their costumes, she used fines fabrics, including Italian silk and Indian cotton. The Italian opera singers at Havana's Tacon Theater were among the best performers in the world, and she had to make sure they were dressed properly. In gratitude, the performers often gave her expensive jewelry.

Antonio and Esterre had been in Cuba for several years when Captain Leopold O'Donnell, the governor-general of Havana, visited them. He announced himself and inquired if this was the home of Superintendent Meucci. Antonio's title at the opera was Superintendent of Mechanism, and he was considered to be something of a wizard with electrical mechanisms. Captain O'Donnell frequented the opera, where he heard about Antonio Meucci.

The captain explained impatiently that he was in charge of a regiment of soldiers, all of whom had problems keeping their metal swords, buckles, and helmets from rusting in Cuba's high heat and humidity. To prevent the rust, they had to send all their metal equipment to France to be electroplated. That was a time-consuming and expensive solution to the problem. O'Donnell asked Antonio if he knew anything about electroplating.

The captain was an imposing figure, a tall, muscled man dressed in a gray uniform and with a sword tucked into its sheath by his side. Cuba was under the colonial rule of Spain in the 1840s and Captain Leopoldo O'Donnell, a Spanish military general was governor of Havana. He was well known as the central figure in the brutal suppression of slave rebellions. Given O'Donnell's reputation and Antonio's own troubled history with men in uniform, Meucci was likely apprehensive about the reason the captain had sought him out. However, he wasted no time in convincing O'Donnell that he knew what electroplating involved.

First invented in 1805 by Italian chemist Luigi Brugnatelli, electroplating is a process for coating items with a thin, permanent wash of metal. These items, typically metallic themselves, are placed in a bath containing a solution of metal salts connected to the negative terminal of a battery. When the electric current is passed through the bath the metals (which are positively charged) are attracted to and deposited on the (negatively charged) item as a solid coating.

Though the captain didn't understand the principle involved, he asked Antonio if he might be able to perform the electroplating treatments right there in Havana. This would save both the time and the costs involved in shipping the gear and armaments back and forth to France. Realizing that the purpose of O'Donnell's visit was legitimate, Antonio pressed O'Donnell for details of what he wanted done, and realized that he could indeed perform the necessary operations on the helmets, belts and swords. However, he would need much better batteries than those available in Havana. In a deposition to the Court many decades later Antonio recounted this experience with electroplating:

> "*I had familiarized myself with galvanoplastic electricity,*" he explained, "*and Captain General O'Donnell was anxious to save expense in galvanizing buttons, sword-hilts and such other things used in the army. I told the general that I could do it at [a] lower price than he was then paying, if I could procure the proper batteries for that purpose. These could not be procured at that time in Havana, but in the year 1844, Gaetano Negretti brought to Havana some galvanic batteries and other electrical supplies that I needed. I opened a factory for this purpose and employed several men – as near as I can remember about 12 or 15. I did not have sufficient batteries for my work, and Mr. Negretti, in a year or two after, sent me further supplies from New York.*"

Antonio drew upon his own observations and studies of the work of other scientists, particularly Luigi Brugnatelli, who was the first to obtain gold-plating by means of electrical current, and Moritz Jacobi, who experimented with copper. The earlier forms of gold plating, however, were not commercially viable because the gold was deposited in the form of a blackish-gray powder, with no shine, and copper was an expensive material with which to experiment. Moritz Jacobi, Antonio's contemporary, could afford copper as he was working in Russia with the benefit of financing by the Czar.

Antonio had to make efficient and productive use of the available materials and had to juggle a number of variables in order to make the electroplating session a success. Though we don't know exactly what metals Antonio used, those most commonly used at the time were antimony, brass, copper, gold, nickel, silver and zinc. Of these, nickel would have been the most effective and inexpensive anti-corrosive coating for the Cuban swords, helmets and buckles. Variations in the amount of current applied, in the temperature, strength and acidity of the bath and distance between the electrodes could all affect the outcome . Antonio testified years later in court, "*I provide myself with the best books and matter concerning electricity.*" Indeed, when he began the electroplating work, Antonio Meucci was following new developments related to electricity throughout Europe, Russia and in the Americas. Antonio read newspapers and books in Italian, French, and Spanish but he never learned English, the native tongue of the country where he lived in the final years of his life. Though he did not put all these developments into use in this episode of his life, they would all figure into his later work — his invention of the telephone.

It was several months before Antonio's new batteries arrived by ship from New York. As soon as he had them in hand, he began to devote all his nights and weekends to the electroplating project, for many swords, buckles and helmets came his way. In the late night hours Antonio spent electroplating swords, he was surrounded by the sounds of guitar and piano music, of singing and dancing coming from many of the houses nearby. Such pleasant, industrious evenings slipped by quickly and years passed, almost without notice. The Meuccis were building toward their future and he was being paid handsomely for his after-hours jobs. For years one could see people lining up outside Antonio's laboratory with their household goods, silverware, and candelabras for him to treat with his "electrical machines."

At this time in the 1840s scientists were exploring ways to manipulate electricity by extending the process of electroplating on an industrial scale and also by developing battery technology — the classic primary cell and secondary cell (or storage) batteries. They were also experimenting with insulation for electrical wire using gutta percha, a natural plastic created by boiling the sap of a gutta tree, for insulating electrical cable. Most impressive of all was the discovery of the telegraph wire with an electric current that Samuel Morse used to stretch across the New York harbor.

The Electric Scream, Illustration by Shirley Trievel

Chapter Six

Electric Shock Treatment

ntonio and Esterre's home, the Gran Teatro de Tacon, became a cultural center in Havana, not only because of the opera, but because it was the site of a series of masked balls. Because the theater had been so costly to build, its owner, Don Francisco, decided to raise money by inaugurating Carnival balls in Havana for everyone, regardless of social class. Although the tickets only cost one dollar in today's economy, money was made by selling drinks.

The night of the Carnival, Thursday, February 18, 1838, 7000 people gathered inside the theater. Because the theater could hold only a fraction of the interested patrons, fifteen thousand others gathered outside. As historian Eduardo Otto described,

> "*The number of people in the streets began to increase, masks of all types were observed….there are rules concerning masks: anyone can enter except for Negroes…*"

Negroes, as the African slaves were called, were excluded because they rebelled against their condition of slavery and there was a prevailing fear of these black-skinned slaves by whites in the Americas in the 1800s. The Carnival festivities, however, grew in popularity among whites after the first one, and eventually were held in February and March and again for nine days during the month of September in all of Havana's neighborhoods. Although we have no record of their attendance, surely Antonio, Esterre and Lorenzo must have celebrated at these events, along with their Italian and Cuban friends.

Because the Gran Teatro de Tacon was a prominent cultural institution in Havana, Antonio and Esterre came into contact with people of all sectors of the Cuban society. In 1848 some physicians in Havana became aware of his reputation and approached him to ask if he could use electric treatments on their patients. Experimentation using electricity for medical purposes began in Antonio's era and such treatment was, and still is, risky. Though he had no medical credentials, Antonio was consulted by medical professionals because he was known to be working at the forefront of discovery of the many different uses of electricity. He was one of a handful of scientists advancing the use of electricity at this point in history, and his laboratory was situated in town where he was accessible to many people who asked for ways electricity could be applied to solve their problems. In his court testimony years later, Antonio described in detail his first experiments on human beings in 1849.

"The idea came to me to apply electricity to sick persons. I devoted myself to giving electrical shocks to various persons employed by me. I laid from my laboratory to a third room an electrical conductor and I produced the electricity by a series of batteries of Bunsen that I kept in my laboratory. One day a person known to me appeared who was sick with rheumatism in the head.

Then I put him in the third room. I put in his hands two conductors, communicating with the battery, and at the end of the conductors there was a utensil made of cork."

What happened next was a pivotal moment in the history of scientific discovery. His affidavit continues: *"In my laboratory, where I kept an instrument identical with the one he held in his hand, I ordered him to put the metal tongue in his mouth. I wished to ascertain where was his disease. I put the same instrument to my ear. The moment that the sick person introduced the little tongue between his lips, he received a discharge and yelled. I obtained, at that same moment, in my ear a sound."*

The instrument Antonio described is illustrated in this figure. Copper wire is wound through the center, feeding into a metallic "tongue" (the outside loop to the

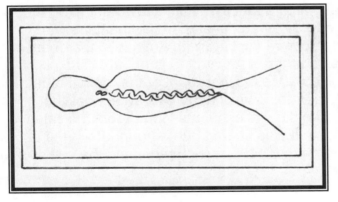

left). The lines surrounding the wound copper wire illustrate the cork hous-

ing, which provides the insulation. The two open lines to the far right indicate the wires going back through the hallway to the batteries. This is the instrument Antonio gave to the patient and he held an identical one in his hand at the other end of the long hallway. On hearing the scream he interrupted the procedure, realizing that the only way he could have heard that sound from the patient was through the wire.

Antonio drew a diagram of the layout of the rooms of this first experiment performed in Havana in 1848.

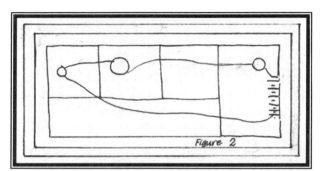

Figure 2

The top of Figure 2 is divided into three rooms, which were part of his apartment and these rooms were looking to the court-yard of the theater (shown as the open rectangle at the bottom of the figure). The batteries (about sixty Bunsen batteries, yielding a total of about 114 volts shown at the right side of the figure) were located in the theater's workshop, which communicated with Antonio's apartment through a door and also with the courtyard. The patient was located in the first room at the top left of the figure, while Antonio was in the workshop near the batteries. The big circle in the second room indicates a reel of wire. It was, in part, the amount of wire, and in part, the battery power which regulated the volt of electricity.

Importantly, during his administration of electric shocks, Antonio had a way to break the circuit of electricity, stopping it before the patient could be hurt. Before experimenting again, he covered the implement with a funnel made of paste-board, shown in the figure 3, to prevent the metal "tongue" from contact with

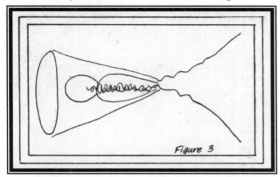

Figure 3

the speaker's flesh, which was the cause of the shock. Antonio goes on to describe how he remedied the problem of the shock:

"I ordered the sick person to repeat the operation made before, and not to have any fear to be affected by the electricity and to speak freely into the funnel. He did so immediately. He put his funnel to his mouth and I put mine to the ear. At the moment that said individual spoke, I received the sound of the word – not distinct – a murmur – an inarticulate sound. Then I tried it again in different days, and I obtained the same result. From this moment…I recognized that I had obtained the transmission of the human word by means of conducting–wire united with several batteries to produce electricity."

This historic event occurred in the spring of 1848, and it marked the first time in recorded history that the human voice was transmitted through wires. During that year Antonio excitedly tried many combinations of ways to reproduce the sound of the speaker. Realizing the value of "tuning down" the electrical charge, he stated in his deposition: *"Experimenting, I found that I didn't need a current so strong as the one produced by many cells; and the current not being too strong, gave better results in the transmission of the sound."* Still he had much more work to do to perfect

what he then referred to as a "speaking telegraph."
Alexander Graham Bell, who is credited with having
made this same discovery, was just two years old at
this time.

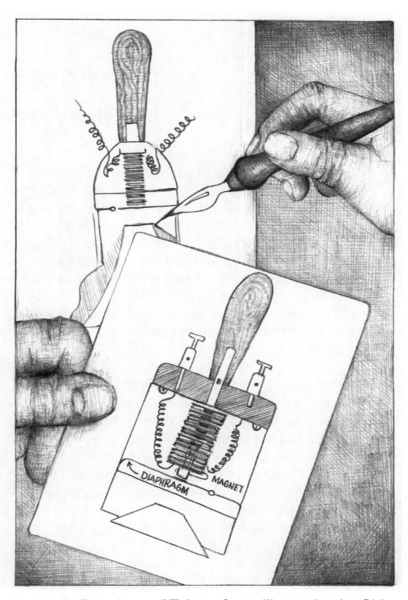

Antonio's Drawings of Telettrofono, Illustration by Shirley Trievel

Chapter Seven

'Telettrofono'

Shortly after Antonio discovered the speaking telegraph, which he referred to as the 'telettrofono' (*tell-eh-tro-fono*) he learned that the Gran Teatro de Tacon was about to close its doors. Don Francisco, owner of the Italian Opera Company, lamented that the Cubans had lost interest in opera. They had gradually stopped attending his theater, and it was no longer a profitable business for him. Rather than yield to defeat, Don Francisco decided to focus on organizing opera performances in New York in the United States.

Things had gone so well for Antonio in Havana that it was difficult to imagine how he could continue his good fortune by leaving. Nevertheless, he began his preparations for departure and packed huge cases with his batteries and other laboratory equipment, knowing that he would be able to find more and better materials for his experiments with the speaking telegraph in New York. Esterre turned her attention to the brighter side, as she counted their savings, which she carefully packed for their trip.

The Meuccis were leaving Cuba with a stash of cash, and Antonio was astonished to learn that they had about $20,000 (a sum equivalent to $500,000 in today's economy). Esterre was smart with money; Antonio was not, and they both knew that. She made him sign a note stating that she was in charge of their finances. Together they agreed to lend their friend Lorenzo a few hundred dollars. Then Esterre extracted a pledge from Antonio. He had to promise to deposit the remaining money in a bank when they got to New York and use it to buy property. Esterre wanted a house of her own when they arrived in their third, and final, country of residence.

On Tuesday, April 23, 1850, the Meuccis' boarded the *Norma*, which had twice as many sails as the *Coccodrillo,* and arrived on New York's bustling shores in just two weeks. They arrived on May 1, 1850, disembarking into one of the world's most densely populated metropolitan areas – a center of commerce, a magnet for immigrants from around the world, a place of immense wealth side-by-side with grinding poverty.

At the time of their arrival in New York in 1850, the place that was to become their home was on the verge of becoming one of the largest cities in the world. It contained all the contrasts of modern life, is worst and best aspects, broad avenues and palaces alongside tenements where men women and children crowded together in festering conditions. Central Park was one of the few places where people of all classes and races mingled, having fun and relaxing together. Within a decade of the Meuccis' arrival in New York, there were a million people in New York, straining the city's public service system. The city experienced disease, fire hazards, and problems providing police protection for the many people who lived there. Beyond the Park borders, tremendous tensions and conflicts developed over who controlled New York and it became a divided city. Individual fortunes were made by a few, while other individuals who were equally deserving, fell on the shoals of destitution.

Antonio was 43 years old when he arrived New York. Neither he nor Esterre spoke more than a few words of English. Yet, soon after their arrival, they found a cottage to buy on tiny, rural Staten Island, just a short ferryboat ride from the southern tip of Manhattan. Their friend Lorenzo joined them in the simple white clapboard house that was to be the Meuccis' home for the rest of their lives. Esterre managed the house and the money and cooked the meals. Without her, the men would not have been able to follow their passions for science and song.

To Antonio, New York seemed filled with possibility. He was one of only a few hundred Italians living there at the time, but only ten years later, in the 1860s, New York City's Italian community was approximately 10,000 people. By the early 1900s, a huge wave of immigration would swell their numbers. Many were peasants and farmers; others were artisans and unskilled workers looking for an opportunity to improve their situation and break free of the yoke of poverty that had been their condition in Italy. But in New York the lodgings of Italians were often run-down, overcrowded apartments with poor sanitary conditions and no hot water, often without heating in the winter or ventilation in the summer. Though their cottage was indeed modest, Antonio lived in luxury compared with most of the Italians in New York living in Little Italy's tenement apartments.

Still, Italians in New York were noticeable for their talent; many were artists and artisans, many were importers. Since opera was the most prominent form of

Italian culture in New York, Antonio, Esterre, and Lorenzo settled quickly into a tight community of their fellow Italians in their new homeland.

One of Antonio's first tasks was to set up his laboratory in the spacious basement of his new home. Equipped with coils and wire and rows of batteries, it was soon ready to be the site of on-going experiments in transmitting the human voice over wires. He devoted himself entirely to these experiments rather than joining the staff of the opera company in New York. His work progressed steadily.

As Antonio explained in his court deposition, *"I took the instrument that I brought from Havana . . . and speaking with my wife, I obtained the same result . . . only I needed to see and know some factory where* were constructed telegraphic instruments, in order to open my mind and be in the knowledge of what was in use." After visiting such a factory and observing the manufacturing process in operation, Antonio constructed a model for a new instrument.

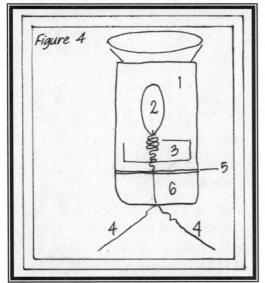

This new instrument (Figure 4) consisted of a tin tube (No 1) at the upper end of which was a mouth-piece, which the speaker was to put directly to his or her mouth, and a metallic tongue (No 2). The center of the device is the one Antonio used when he conducted the electric shock treatment, and here he built a housing to better conduct the sound of the voice.

Antonio refined his design after he had purchased some telegraphic instruments for study. He tested both pasteboard and wood to see which functioned best for the housing, and he added three new refinements. The first was a bobbin or core with coils and the second was an iron diaphragm. The third innovation was to place in the interior a small tongue of platinum soldered to a conductor of copper, thereby "communicating" with the battery. Finally, he had a model that produced satisfactory results.

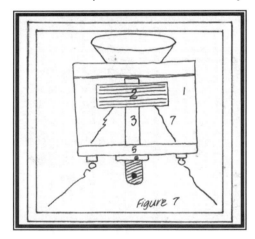
Figure 7

This drawing reproduced from Meucci's legal deposition (Figure 7) indicates the bobbin and core mechanism. Antonio's goal was to make his transmissions as clear as possible, and his experiments focused on how best to reproduce the range of vibrations that the human voice produces. In this diagram: #1 represents a pasteboard box, with a wooden bottom; #2 a bobbin; #3 a steel bar, tempered and permanently magnetized, passing through the center of the bobbin, which can be raised and lowered by means of a screw at the bottom; #4 (the thin line above #2) an animal diaphragm, with a hole in the center, with a metallic tongue of iron under it, serving as a valve; #5 the bottom of the instrument in wood; #6 (directly below #5) a nut to raise and lower the center of the bobbin. Insulated copper wire comes from the bobbin, passing through the bottom of the instrument to the left and right at the bottom of the diagram, to connect with the battery.

The center of the bobbin produced an electromagnetic current, which is why Antonio put the magnet and bobbin in this instrument. By placing the

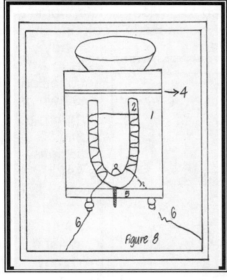

Figure 8

magnetized steel bar higher or lower in the bobbin, or nearer or further from the diaphragm, it produced the oscillations of the membrane on the top, which formed the voice. In the cases when he used animal or vegetable substances as the membrane, he obtained greater elasticity than an iron membrane, but needed to put the central bar at greater distance from the membrane. When using an iron diaphragm, he needed to put the steel bar closer to it, for it was less elastic and needed more current to make it oscillate.

In the model illustrated here in Fig. 8, Antonio experimented with circular forms of magnetized steel. The horseshoe better held the electrical current. This diagram shows a cylindrical box of pasteboard (#1), above the mouthpiece, to speak in, with a cover enclosing the membrane. The difference is #2, the steel horseshoe, tempered and permanently magnetized, kept in the center by a screw (#3) to the bottom of the instrument. The membrane (#4) was sometimes metal and sometimes animal substance, a fabric of different qualities such as parchment paper saturated with paraffin (wax and then passed through plumbago (a herbal plant often used as lubricant). The bottom block (#5) and insulated copper wire (#6) surrounded the two branches of the horseshoe to form a helix.

During the years he worked to devise his telephonic instruments, Esterre grew increasingly weak and un-

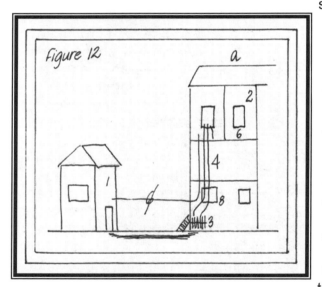

steady from a condition known as rheumatoid arthritis. Antonio knew that he had to stay close at hand, in case she needed help getting out of bed or navi-gating the stairs. It occurred to him to use the 'telettrofono' to communicate with Esterre when he was not upstairs in their room. In order to modify his invention to suit this new need he made a drawing [Figure 12] of his proposed two-way telephone installation, which included a wide separation between the line designated to go from Antonio to Esterre and the line that would bring her voice back to him. This separation was necessary to prevent an echo of the speaker's own voice. Then Antonio installed the world's first-ever telephone link at his Staten Island home.

The new 'telettrofono' quickly became a household necessity, as Esterre's arthritis grew worse and she was unable to move for several hours at a time. Though he tried, Antonio could not cure her with his electric treatments, but he could stay in very close touch with her. He put a permanent 'telettrofono' line between the basement and her bedroom on the second floor, then he extended it out to his laboratory in a side building, so he could also call her from there. Sadly, no record was made of the exact date they first spoke on the instrument or what they said to one another, but it *is* a matter of record that the very first telephone conversation ever held was between Esterre and Antonio Meucci. Their home was the site of the telephone's first use.

Flickering Flame, Illustration by Shirley Trievel

Chapter Eight

Candles and Paper

I n July 30, 1850, months after Antonio and Esterre settled in to their new home, the *New York Tribune* published an announcement that caused a stir throughout the city and set the Italian community abuzz with excitement: *"This morning the ship Waterloo arrived from Liverpool with aboard Giuseppe Garibaldi, man of world fame, hero and defender of Rome. He will be welcomed by all who know him in keeping with this gallant character and the services he has rendered in the cause of liberty."*

Giuseppe Garibaldi (*Gee-oo-sep-pee Gare-ee-baldy*), whose most striking physical features were his red-blond beard and calm but penetrating eyes, had become a legend in his own lifetime. After losing a major battle to defend Rome against the French, General

> Both Italy and America were caught up in civil wars in the mid 1800s. The struggle for nationhood in Italy, called the Rigorsmento, was led by Giuseppe Gar-ibaldi, whose army drove out the French Bourbons and Austrians from Italy and united the north and south regions of that county into one nation. Many foreign soldiers, including many Americans, enlisted as volunteers in General Garibaldi's army.

Garibaldi had to flee Italy in fear of his life. Garibaldi began a five-year exile, one year of which was spent in the home of Antonio and Esterre.

Antonio was initially part of the committee that waited on the dock to welcome this famous Italian patriot and exile. Somehow, Antonio managed to be the first of the group to invite the hero to come live in his home. Garibaldi accepted. He had arrived in New York suffering from arthritis pains so severe they almost paralyzed him. Like Esterre, he needed to convalesce for hours at a time, and he was much in need of a quiet place to rest.

Esterre insisted that they make Garibaldi's room beautiful. Whenever she felt well enough, she sewed curtains and bedding for the modest upstairs room. Equally excited, Antonio set aside his experiments with the '*telettrofono*' in order to exercise another of his many skills. He designed and built the best furniture he could, given the material available to him. The rocking chair he fashioned from branches can still be seen at his home along with a piano he built with glass keys.

New York's Italian community had planned a huge reception for General Garibaldi, but at the last minute he proved to be too sick to attend. His simple note declining their invitation: *"Gentlemen, I regret that I must tell you that my poor health continues and will make it impossible for me to take part in the public gathering that you are planning for Saturday next. I would prefer to quietly and humbly become a citizen of this great republic of free men, and pursue a career that would permit me to earn my bread and await a more favorable moment to return to Italy to liberate it from its oppressors.*" Indeed, Giuseppe Garibaldi was relieved to have been taken to the home of the Meuccis for his rest and recovery. As soon as Giuseppe was settled in, Antonio returned to his experiments, but he grew concerned that the general had no meaningful work to do. And indeed, the longer Garibaldi rested the more restless he became.

One day, while Antonio was working in his laboratory and Esterre was busy in the house, Garibaldi decided to go hunting. He snatched up a musket (which resembles a rifle), put on his boots and went to the island of Manhattan where he wandered along the creeks and through the fields. In 1850 Manhattan had many very crowded neighborhoods, but they were small by today's standards and there was still plenty of open space, where Giuseppe found rabbits and foxes to hunt. He had only been gone an hour or so when the police brought him back to Antonio's door. They had arrested one of the world's most famous fighters for hunting "out of season." Antonio took his guest back into the house and promised the police he would keep the hero out of trouble, vowing to find something constructive for his friend to do.

Determined to devise some venture to employ Garibaldi, Antonio and Lorenzo joined together to developed a business plan. They decided to make and sell candles. The electric light bulb had not yet been invented, and homes and businesses alike depended on candles, kerosene lamps, and gas lamps for illumination. There was always a market for candles. Theirs proved to be no ordinary candle-making factory. Antonio devised a method of distilling residue from coal to be mixed with paraffin and he refined the molding process of candles made of paraffin by saturating the mold with whale sperm oil or linseed oil, so that the candles came out of the mold with great ease. He then developed a special candlewick that burned clean and bright – at the time, most other wicks gave off a black carbon residue. Antonio built a furnace in the backyard and set Giuseppe to work. When resting from work, Giuseppe Garibaldi enjoyed fishing and Antonio bought a fishing boat, painted it red, white and green – the colors of the nation of Italy. In his memoirs, Garibaldi gave no indication that he suspected the candle factory had been devised with him in mind. He wrote, *"A friend of mine, Antonio Meucci, Florentine and a good and kindly man, decided to found a candle factory and he asked me to help. I worked several months with Meucci."*

Giuseppe stayed with Antonio and Esterre, from October 1850 until April 1851. He left Staten Island for Peru, where he worked, as he had in his youth, as a ship's captain. In 1854, he was allowed to return to Italy, where he was responsible for most of the military victories leading to the unification of Italy. Fondly recalling his days in Staten Island in his memoirs, Garibaldi wrote, *"My dearest boss Meucci, a fine man, did not treat me as one of his working men but as one of the family and with much affection, like Signora Esterre, his wife. There was no luxury in the home, but no life necessity was lacking, either lodging or food. Meucci paid my expenses, amounting to a considerable amount of money."*

After Garibaldi's departure, Antonio's inventive mind took on a new project. Having discovered a new way of making candles, he turned his gaze on another daily essential – paper. As it had been for centuries, in the 1850s the main ingredient in paper was rags.

When Antonio read about failed attempts to make paper from wood pulp, he decided to take up the challenge. The candle-making operation was successfully underway, and the *'telettrofono'* was fully functional in the Meucci home. Antonio was free to creating a wood pulp rich enough in fibers and filaments to give it the right consistency and strength to make high quality paper.

Previous attempts to make paper from wood had involved grinding the wood into a sawdust-like powder, to which ground rags had to be added for strength and elasticity. Antonio discovered a way to remove the "gummy" substances from the long fibers of wood and vegetables, making it possible to use the fibers in long filaments rather than having to reduce them to powder. Paper made from these filaments needed no rags at all. He also developed a new chemical process that lightened the color of the paper so that whatever was written on it could be more easily read.

These were notable advances in the history of papermaking, and Antonio became known for his discoveries. His innovations caught the interest of the general manager of the Associated Press, David Craig. Always looking for better paper on which to print his newspapers, Craig agreed to pay Antonio $10,000 a month to set up a paper processing plant in the state of Ohio. Knowing that his reliable friends were close by, and could see to Esterre's care, he agreed to try it out. He packed his suitcase and left the cottage on Staten Island in the summer of 1865 to set up the plant.

Within months of its opening the Ohio plant was forced to close down. The long, bloody Civil War in the U.S. ended in May of 1865, throwing the economy into shambles. Several of the paper plant's investors were in a financial crisis because they had also invested in guns and weapons, which were suddenly no longer in great demand. When they went bankrupt, the plant no longer had financing. Although the war's end was a very good thing – marking the end of slavery and the beginning of healing a divided nation – Antonio was out of a job.

He never saw his technique of making paper from wood actually manufactured. Instead, he was paid a mere $75 for his efforts to set up the plant and offered a $20 a week job. The job, at another paper plant, this one in New Jersey, lasted only 6 months, and when it ended Antonio returned home to Esterre, after having been gone almost a year.

Harper Magazine Illustration of Ferryboat Westfield
Accident

Chapter Nine

Explosion on the Staten Island Ferry

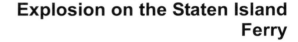

By the time Antonio returned home from Ohio and New Jersey, Esterre's rheumatoid arthritis had advanced to the point that she seldom left her upstairs bedroom. Antonio hired a woman named Maria Ciuci to be a helper in the house beginning October 22, 1865. Every day, the three of them used the *telettrofono* to communicate with one another. Curious neighbors overheard these conversations, and asked if they, too, could try out the telephonic implements. Maria Ciuci would later testify in court in support of Antonio's claims about the use of the telephone in his home and with neighbors. She recalled that they said, "*Good morning, fine day*" and such.

Antonio continued to improve the *telettrofono.* He had made twelve different models before finally deciding that the instrument was ready to introduce to the world. The diagram here depicts the internal

Diagram published in *New York Electrical World* November 28, 1885 of Meucci's model from 1864.

operating mechanism of Antonio's best model.

But before he could take the first steps to launch his great discovery, disaster struck. One day in August 1871, Antonio boarded the ferryboat *Westfield*, bound from Manhattan to Staten Island. Almost all the passengers were outside on deck, enjoying the balmy summer weather in the harbor, when they heard an immense noise. The water boilers that provided the steam that powered the ferry's engine exploded and were spewing boiling water into the air.

Passengers tried desperately to evade the lethal geyser, but there was nowhere to run. Antonio was standing where boiling water poured down on him; then he passed out. He awoke days later in the hospital with burns over much of his face and body. He learned that more than one hundred people died in the explosion. After he returned home, it would still be many weeks before he recuperated completely from his injuries. Although Esterre was no doubt relieved to see her husband home and on the mend, she was also growing increasingly concerned over how to pay their bills. All the money they brought with them from Havana was now gone.

Maria, who now was taking care of both Esterre and Antonio, suggested to Esterre that they look for someone who would buy the "talking instruments." Utterly distraught about their dwindling finances, Esterre encouraged Maria to find a buyer, though neither woman realized the value of the models. Maria eventually sold Antonio's *telettrofono* to a second-hand dealer named John Flemming.

As the days passed, Antonio slowly grew stronger and his burns and other injuries healed. The first day that he was able to get out of bed, he walked slowly around the ground floor of the house and eventually out to his work building. Thinking he would call Esterre, he noticed that the *telettrofono* wasn't in its usual place. Haltingly, he climbed the stairs to ask Esterre what had happened to it. When she admitted that the models had been sold weeks ago to keep up with the expenses, Antonio couldn't believe things had really been so bad that she had to sell his greatest work. Why hadn't she told him they needed money so badly?! They could easily have sold the candles or the piano that Antonio made. Why his *telettrofono*, of all things? Esterre knew what the *telettrofono* meant to Antonio, though neither of them really understood what it would eventually mean to the world. She simply had lost patience with his years of experiments on a device that yielded no profit.

Still weak from his bodily injuries, Antonio's spirit was now being tested. His friends, Giuseppe and Lorenzo, had left and his wife no longer believed in his finest experiment. His fortunes, once so bright, were flickering out like a candle flame, leaving no trace of anything he had ever done. Although he had been granted patents for his inventions with paper and candles, he assigned them to be looked after by his associates whom he trusted and whom he considered more business savvy than he was himself. But he never saw profits from these inventions either. Instead of yielding to defeat, Antonio decided to get busy reconstructing *telettrofono* models. He was hoping to stay on course with his pre-explosion plans to present his speaking telegraph invention to the U.S. Patent

Office and to seek financial backing for starting a *telettrofono* company.

All that summer and fall, Antonio worked in a frenzy to reconstruct the models and refine his drawings so that other people could also understand them. At that time, very few people knew enough about chemistry, electricity or mechanics to comprehend how all three of these elements came together to create the *telettrofono*. When Antonio was satisfied with his new models, his next step was to convince potential partners to invest in producing the implements on a large scale. It was time to introduce the *telettrofono* into broader use, using existing telegraph wires.

Antonio Meucci, Illustration by Shirley Trievel

Chapter Ten

The Patent Business

Describing his efforts to introduce the *telettro-fono* to the world in 1871, Antonio said in his court testimony, *"I prepared a description and specifications of my inventions, and took them to Mr. A Bertolino, who went with me as a friend and inter-preter to Mr. Thomas D. Stetson, a patent lawyer. Mr. Bertolino interpreted for me and we gave to Mr. Stetson the drawing that I had mentioned."*

Thomas D. Stetson was a New York patent officer, vis-ited by Antonio and his friend Bertolino, who went to-gether to apply for a patent for the *telettrofono*. A pat-ent confers special rights of ownership of the inven-tion, which is considered the exclusive property of the patent holder. Antonio told Stetson that he wanted to patent the *telettrofono* and was planning to raise the patent fee of $250, far more than Antonio had after his disasters. But Stetson was unreceptive. After review-ing Antonio's submissions, he sent a letter saying, *"Your telegraphing will have to be experimented with considerably before it will be ready for a pat-ent. I advise making a good many experiments, to prove the reality of the thing. When you have got things to suit you, I wish to see the experiments, I will come down and stop a night at your house, if you will keep me and show me all about it."*

Stetson's proposed visit never happened. Antonio ex-plained why in his court testimony several years later:

"It is true that he would come to make experiments. I could not accept; first, for my wife's sickness; second, I had no bed for him to sleep in; third because I had no money to entertain him; and then my wife was so tired of telephonic experiments that she told me to go and make them elsewhere, and not in this house." So although Antonio vowed to continue his quest for a full patent, he was forced to accept Stetson's offer of a $20 temporary patent called a "caveat" instead. He left his drawings at Stetson's patent office.

Since Esterre didn't want any more telephonic experiments in their home, Antonio proceeded straight away to see if he could set up the *'telettrofono'* demonstration for Stetson at the American District Telegraph Company instead. In the summer of 1872 he contacted a Mr. Grant, the company's vice president. Antonio stated in his affidavit, *"I told Mr. Grant that I had an invention for talking over wire that I called the 'Sound Telegraph.' I explained the principles of the invention to him, gave him my drawings, plans and specifications, and he promised to furnish the wire and lines to try my instruments and also to assist me in making a practical test of the invention. I told Mr. Grant that I had two rough specimens that we could try. I frequently went to see him for a year and a half. Each time that I visited him he made promises of help, until about two years after my first visit, when he told me that he had lost the papers and would have nothing to do with it."*

Grant may truly have lost Antonio's diagrams, as he claimed. More likely he kept Antonio's papers and turned them over to his American Telegraph Company electricians to test. American District Telegraph Company was part of the Western Union group of telegraph companies, and the place offering a million dollars to anyone who could devise a system of telegraphing multiple messages over the same telegraph wire.

Taking up the challenge was Scottish-born Alexander Graham Bell. He was twenty-eight years old then and had recently been appointed professor of vocal physiology at Boston University, having spent his adult life as a teacher of the deaf. His work as a teacher had led him to an interest in the transmission of harmonic vibrations. Another scientist, Elishu Gray, worked at Western Union affiliate. He was a rival to Bell, as they were both racing to be the first to electronically transmit vibrations produced by the notes of the musical scale. Their efforts were aimed at winning the competition for $1 million by Western Union for the development of a system of electro-harmonic telegraph as a means of increasing the number of messages that could be sent at the same time over a single telegraph wire. Telegraph companies were looking for ways to increase their message-carrying capabilities on the lines they had, rather than constructing new and expensive telegraph lines. During the same time Bell and Gray were in a neck-and-neck race for this prize, they both apparently experimented with models of the telephone.

Four years after Antonio gave his drawings to Mr. Grant, on February 14, 1876 Alexander Graham Bell entered the U.S. Patent Office in Washington, D.C. and submitted his application for the patent for the telephone. Elisha Gray arrived at the same office on the same day and submitted *his* application for a caveat on an instrument almost identical to the one described in Bell's application, only more detailed in its description. And although Bell had no working model of the telephone at the time, he was granted the patent for his application. The first model of the telephone that Bell used in public to successfully transmit the human voice was an electro-magnetic device, the same as the Meucci telephone.

This move on the part of Alexander Graham Bell dealt Antonio a crushing defeat. Alexander Graham Bell was granted the patent for the telephone, one month after his application and after many visits to the Patent Office by Bell's influential father-in-law and lawyers.

"About the year 1876," Antonio testified, *"reading a newspaper sent to me by a friend, I saw that the patent for the invention of the telephone had been granted to a certain A. Bell. I recognized immediately that my invention had been stolen, the fruit of many years of labor, because the description was exactly identical with the one I had made. I caused Mr. Bertolino to write a letter to Mr. Stetson, begging him to inform the Patent Office that the invention had been stolen from me. Mr. Stetson said that he would have done it, but I believe that, as I had no money to give him, he didn't pay any attention to it."*

Getting no satisfaction from the Patent Office, Antonio turned his attention to Alexander Graham Bell and wrote to him several times but never received a reply. Bell was busy demonstrating his telephone at the grand Centennial Exposition in Philadelphia where he was visited by the emperor of Brazil. The emperor, Pedro II was the first person to try out Bell's telephone, proclaiming, *"My God, It talks!"* Newspaper reporters caught his words and soon the world knew about this new invention, opening the way for fame and riches for Alexander Graham Bell.

Meanwhile, Antonio had found several investors to form his own telephone company but Antonio's newly developed *'telettrofono'* company, called the Globe Telephone Company, did not have a chance to manufacture telephones. Instead they were busy petitioning the U.S. government to cancel the Bell patent for the telephone. The patent granted Bell exclusive rights to exploit the invention for commercial purposes, which meant that Antonio could not commercialize his invention. In response to the lawsuit by Globe Telephone Company, Bell's newly formed American Bell Telephone Company immediately counter-sued.

In the years that followed hundreds of pages of depositions were taken which consumed Antonio's life. He was on the defensive in an effort to claim his priority on the telephone invention. Meucci was certainly not the first person to have conceived the notion of transmitting voice through electrically charged wire. He was, however, the first to apply for a patent for the device, having developed the instrument over more than twenty years of experimentation.

Irregularities occurred at the U.S. Patent Office when the legal case for the Meucci-Bell lawsuit was being prepared. The material submitted by Antonio Meucci in 1871 to the patent office could no longer be found there. That is, his drawings and description of how the 'telettrofono' worked had disappeared. All that remained was the patent register with the number and description of the caveat for the Speaking Telegraph given to Antonio Meucci, by the office. Worse still, the U.S. Circuit Court in New York decided this case between Meucci and Bell in 1887, in favor of Alexander Graham Bell, a grave miscarriage of justice.

In subsequent years many other lawsuits were brought against the Bell patent, some by the United States government itself, but the Bell Telephone Company had by then become an empire. Western Union, on behalf of Elisha Gray, also sued the American Bell Telephone Company, when Gray claimed that Alexander Graham Bell had obtained his telephone patent by fraud. Interestingly, Bell's company settled out of court with Western Union, paying them a handsome sum to drop the lawsuit. No such settlement was offered to Antonio Meucci, however.

In 1887 when the court judgment struck him down, Antonio was 79 years old. During the years he had been fighting for recognition as the inventor of the *telettrofono*, Esterre had grown increasingly weak and she died in 1884. A friend of the family testified, "*During the last five years of her life she never moved from her chair, unless she was lifted out. She could not lie down.*" He had also received letters informing him that his friends Lorenzo and Giuseppe had died in Italy. In a letter to Giuseppe Garibaldi's daughter, he wrote, "*I would like to see my rights as inventor recognized before my death.*" He repeated the same wish in a letter to his brother in Italy, but his wish was not to be granted. Antonio died at the age of 81 in 1889, in his Staten Island home.

Two years before his death, on August 22, 1887, the Globe Telephone Company and Antonio Meucci appealed the New York court decision to the Supreme Court of the United States. The U.S. Supreme Court deemed the case worthy of hearing, and scheduled it to be held in October of 1891. But the case was never heard, as the Globe Telephone Company did not pursue the hearing after Antonio's death.

The story of Antonio Meucci has been kept alive by a small group of Italian Americans dedicated to his cause. His home has been preserved in Staten Island, and exists today as the Garibaldi-Meucci Museum. Both Antonio and Esterre are buried on the grounds. In the museum, one can see the chair Antonio made for Garibaldi, the piano he made with glass keys, the candle-making kiln and the remaining models of the *'telettrofono.'*

Photograph of Antonio Meucci—Original in "Museo del Risorgimento", Milan, Italy (Courtesy of Garibaldi-Meucci Museum)

Photograph of Antonio Meucci in his home on Staten Island (Courtesy of Garibaldi-Meucci Museum)

Photographs of Antonio Meucci—(Courtesy of
Garibaldi-Meucci Museum)

Meucci's Telephone Model Re-
productions in the Garibaldi-
Meucci Museum—Photo taken
by Sandra Meucci

Photo of Meucci's Piano with Glass keys in Garibaldi-Meucci Museum (Photograph taken by Sandra Meucci)

Photo of Chair made by Antonio Meucci out of Tree Branches in Garibaldi-Meucci Museum (Photograph taken by Sandra Meucci)

Timeline
Inventions and Significant Life Events of Antonio Meucci

April 13, 1808

Antonio Meucci born at 5 am in Florence, Italy, in S. Frediano quarter, registered with the parish of Castello, in 473 Via Chiara.

November 27, 1821

At the age of 13 Antonio was admitted to the Accademia di Belle Arti (The Academy of Fine Arts) of Florence, at the school of the Elements of Drawing.

Summer 1823

Amatis Meucci, Antonio's father, secured a position for his son as Gatekeeper Superannuary in Florence, Italy. The position allowed Antonio to continue his studies at the Accademia.

October 3, 1823

Antionio began work at the gates of Florence at the age of 16, on June 18, 1824 he was

	promoted to Assistant Gate-keeper, assigned to guard the Porta S. Niccolo (St. Nicolas Gate), which was a forty-five minute walk from his home.
April 1825	Antonio is assigned to light the fire-works at the celebration for the forthcoming birth of a child to Grand Duchess Marie Caroline of Saxony.
May 16, 1825	Report of Auditor Director of Florence of an incident occurring on April 4, 1825, with the fireworks where "...a great deal of rockets shot off from the merlons of the Palazzo Vecchio at various intervals, and many each time rapidly and violently slithering down like thunderbolts and landing on the various spots where spectators were standing..." Antonio Meucci was identified as bearing responsibility along with two other Assistant Gatekeepers.
June 9, 1825	Antonio began his five-day prison sentence under orders of the Buon Governo, for having forgotten to nail down a wooden platform covering an open pit.
January 1829	Antonio completed his studies

at the Accademia's Conservatorio d' Arti e Mestieri in the school of chemistry and mechanics.

October 1833

Antonio seeks and obtains employment as an engineer or technician at the Teatro della Pergola in Florence. He worked at the theater to 1835 under Alessandro Lanari. In July 1834 he became Lanari's confidential assistant.

August 7, 1834

Antonio Meucci and Esterre Mochi marry in the church of Santa Maria Novella, Florence, Italy.

October 5, 1835

The Sardinian Brig *Coccodrillo* departed from the Port of Livorno sailing to the Port of Havana. The Italian Opera Company, including Antonio and Esterri Meucci was on board.

December 16,1835

Don Francisco Marty (impresario of Gran Teatro de Tacon) greeted Antonio and Esterre Meucci upon their arrival in Havana.

December 1835

Don Manual Pastor engages Antonio Meucci in the reconstruction of filters for the public water system in Havana. This marks Antonio's first technical achievement in the city, one that purified the water, making it usable for the public.

February 24, 1836 The construction of the Gran Teatro de Tacon was authorized and in the early spring 1838 the apartments in the annex of the theater (Antonio and Esterre's home) were completed. Antonio diverted a tributary of a nearby river under the theater, to construct a resonance chamber thereby improving the acoustics.

Early 1844 New Spanish Governor Leopoldo O'Donnell approached Antonio about beginning a business of electroplating swords, buckles and helmets for his soldiers.

Spring 1848 Antonio administered an electric shock treatment to a patient when he heard the man scream over the electrified wires. His drawing of the rooms in which he conducted the experiment was done. From this point until 1871 he experimented with the *telettrofono,* or the first telephone.

April 23, 1850	The ship *Norma* disembarks from the Port of Havana and sailed to the Port of Manhattan in New York. The Meucci's leave their home in Cuba.
May 1, 1850	The Meucci's arrive in New York and immediately seek to purchase a home.
July 30, 1850	The ship *Waterloo* arrived to Manhattan from Liverpool, England with Giuseppe Garibaldi on board. Garibaldi moved to the home of Esterre and Antonio Meucci in October 1850, where he lived until April 1851.
January 25, 1859	Patent for Antonio Meucci's candle mold was granted.
April 9, 1859	Caveat for Antonio Meucci's galvanic battery was issued.
September 9, 1862	Patent for Antonio Meucci's improvements in treating mineral oils for paint.
March 13, 1866	Patent for Antonio Meucci's treatment of vegetable fibre for paper pulp was granted.
August 1871	Explosion on Steamboat *Westerfield* fatally wounded more than one hundred people

and Antonio Meucci was seriously burned and injured in the explosion.

December 28, 1871   Caveat for Antonio Meucci's 'sound telegraph" (telephone) was issued. It was renewed in 1872 and 1873.

October 10. 1876   Patent for Antonio Meucci's hygrometer was granted.

October 9, 1885   Antonio Meucci begins his testimony in the U.S. Circuit Court Case Bell/Globe, for the trial that began December 7, 1885.

July 19, 1887   Judge Wallace of the U.S. Circuit Court, for the Southern District of New York, decided the case of Bell/Globe in favor of Bell.

October 18,188   Antonio Meucci died in his home.

Timeline
Western Inventions around the 19th Century

1780: *Luigi Galvani (Italy)* accidentally discovers that the leg of a dead frog twitches when touched with an electrically charged scalpel. He begins to develop his theories of "animal electricity, paving the way for the developments leading to all electrical batteries. *This discovery was the starting point for Antonio Meucci's scientific investigation into the properties of electricity.*

1793: *Claude Chappe (France)* persuades the French government to install a series of towers from which semaphore signals could be relayed from point to point throughout the country. This was the first long-distance telecommunication network in Europe and was copied in Great Britain and the United States.

1800: *Alessandro Volta (Italy)* develops the voltaic pile, a forerunner of the electric battery. It is made of a stack of alternating zinc and silver discs held apart by cloth soaked in salt solution, and provides the first means of producing electricity when and where it is wanted. *Antonio perfected the use of voltaic batteries.*

1805: *Luigi Gasparo Brugnatelli (Italy)* invents the process of electroplating, the art of coating an object with a thin film or a powder of metal by means of an electric current passing through a solution in which the metal and the object to be coated are suspended. *Antonio used this electroplating technique while in Havana, Cuba.*

1807: **Robert Fulton (USA)** builds on the work of James Watt (Scotland) and John Fitch (USA), Fulton and launches the first commercially viable steamboat. *The steamboat however was a dangerous form of travel as illustrated by the explosion on the U.S. Westerfield described in Chapter 9.*

1810: **Giovanni Zamboni (Italy)** a physics professor from Verona, Italy began constructing a dry battery, which he finished in 1812. The battery's electromotive force resulted from chemical reactions between the tin being oxidized and the black oxide of manganese being reduced. Paper acted as a damp conductor.

1816: **Francis Ronalds (England)** builds the first working electric telegraph.

1819: **Hans Christian Oersted (Denmark)** gives birth to the study of electricity and magnetism when he observes that a magnetic needle is deflected at right angles to a wire carrying an electric current – thus discovering the existence of the magnetic field.

1820: **André Ampère (France)** is the first to observe the phenomenon of electromagnetic reaction: if a current is passed through a conductor located in a magnetic field, the field exerts a mechanical force on it. This is the first of two principles that will underlie the development of generators and motors (See Faraday, 1831). He devises the galvanometer to measure electric current and names it after Luigi Galvani, an Italian pioneer in the study of electricity.

1820: **J.F. Daniell (England):** Hygrometer. This is an instrument to measure the relative humidity in the air.

Antonio perfected this instrument, for which he received a patent in 1876.

1821: **Michael Faraday (England)** builds on Oersted's work and plots the magnetic field around a conductor carrying an electric current.

1823: **André Marie Ampère (France)** publishes his first book on electrodynamic theory and his views on the relationship of electricity and magnetism. (The ampere, the unit of electric current, is named after him.)

1823: **William Sturgeon (England)** invents the first electromagnet, in which a current is passed through a coil of insulated wire to induce a strong magnetic field. *Antonio's experiments with permanently magnetized steel rods in the telettrofono were informed by the work of Sturgeon and Ampère.*

1825: **George Stephenson's (England)** invention, Locomotion No. 1, becomes the first steam engine to carry passengers and freight on a regular basis.

1826: **George Simon Ohm (Germany)** formulates the basic law of current flow. Ohm's law describes the relationship between current, electromotive force, and resistance. (The unit of electrical resistance was named the ohm in his honor.) *Theories of resistance and variable resistance underlie the Meucci telephone.*

1829: **Barthélemy Thimonnier (France)** builds the first practical sewing machine, which employs a hook-tipped needle that is moved downward by a foot treadle to produce a chain stitch. *This machine was*

*not commercially available during the time Esterre
was chief seamstress and dressmaker with the Italian
Opera Company*

1830: **Joseph Henry (USA)** discovers the principle of
electromagnetic induction (the fact that a current is
produced in a wire when it is moved near a magnet).

1831: **Michael Faraday (England)** states his Law of
Induction and publishes his discovery of electromagnetic induction. This discovery explains how mechanical motion could be converted into electric energy and
how electric and magnetic effects result from lines of
force that surround conductors and magnets. This is
the second of the two related principles underlying the
development of generators and motors (see Ampere,
1820) and *underlying the inductive loading process
developed in the Meucci telephone.*

1831: **Joseph Henry (USA)** constructs the first practical electromagnetic telegraph.

1832: **Charles *Babbage (England)*** designs the Difference Engine (to do mathematical equations) and
the Analytical Engine (intended to use punched cards
to store instructions and perform calculations – the
first digital computer).

1835: **Samuel Morse (USA)** develops Morse code, a
system of dots (short burst of electricity) and dashes
(longer burst of electricity) corresponding to letters of
the alphabet and numbers, used to transmit messages by wire.

1836: **Samuel Morse (USA)/ Sir Charles Wheat-
stone and Sir William Cooke (England):** In the

same year, inventors on both sides of the Atlantic produce prototypes for electric instruments for telegraphic transmission. Morse's instrument employed an electric switch, activated by finger pressure that turns current on and off. The British version (perfected in 1845 and adopted throughout England) employed a single needle.

1839: **William Grove (England)** built the first battery to use an acid depolarizer (nitric acid), which was later known as the Bunsen Battery. Bunsen Batteries produced high voltage at 1.9 volts. *Antonio Meucci used this battery in his first experiments with the telettrofono in Havana, Cuba.*

1840: **Giovanni Battista Amici (Italy)** invents the oil immersion microscope, leading to the development of microscopes that can enlarge up to 6,000 times, greatly facilitating the new field of cell biology.

1842-3: **Samuel Morse (USA)** stretches a wire across New York harbor and sends an electric current through it. He is awarded $30,000 from Congress toward construction of a telegraph system.

1843: German manufacturers begin using ground wood pulp instead of linen rags to manufacture paper. This is a mechanical process rather than a chemical process.

1844: The first American telegraph line is completed. It stretches 37 miles from Baltimore, Maryland, to Washington, DC. Samuel Morse (USA) sends the first message: "What hath God wrought." *The telegraph wire was an essential component to later development of long –distance telephone use.*

1846: **Elias Howe (USA)** patents the first lockstitch sewing machine. Isaac Merrit Singer (USA) patents a similar machine in 1851 and Howe sues him for patent infringement.

1847: **Ignaz Philipp Semmelweis (Austria)** discovers that if he washes his hands between before and after treating each patient in a hospital, the number of patient deaths from infection is greatly reduced. Few other doctors copy him.

1850: **John and Jacob Brett (England)** lay the first telegraph cable between England and France. A fisherman, mistaking the cable for seaweed, cuts it. It is replaced by armored cable in 1851.

1853: **Manufacturers in England** begin using wood pulp instead of linen rags for papermaking. *Antonio Meucci develops the process of using wood fibers, making an even stronger paper fiber in 1866.*

1854*: **Charles Bourseul (France)** envisioned that speech could be transmitted by electricity and published papers describing the principle.

1854: **John Snow (England)** is the first to understand that contaminated drinking water is the cause of cholera. He stops an epidemic by removing the pump handle from a tainted municipal well.

1854-1866: **Cyrus Field (USA)** in collaboration with others investors, form the Atlantic Telegraph Company, laying a trans-Atlantic telegraph cable.

1859: **Charles Darwin (England)** publishes *On the Origin of Species by Means of Natural Selection,* which explains his ideas on natural selection and revolutionizes the field of biology.

1859: *Gaston Planté (France)* invents the lead-acid rechargeable storage battery, the type widely used in vehicles today.

1859: *Gustav Kirchhoff and Robert Wilhelm Bunsen (Germany)* develop the modern prism spectroscope and apply it to chemical analysis. Each chemical element has its own chemical spectrum, and the spectroscope makes it possible to know the chemical make up of distant phenomena such as the sun and stars by analyzing the light they emit.

1859-60: *Jean Joseph Étienne Lenoir (France)* invents the first workable internal combustion engine, which uses compressed coal gas as fuel and included a battery for storing electricity for ignition. He patents the device and hitches it to a small vehicle, the first "horseless carriage."

1859: *Antonio Meucci (USA)* receives patent for improvements to the process of manufacturing of candles.

1861: Telegraph lines connect New York City and San Francisco.

1863: *Philipp Reis (Germany)* builds his third model of a telephone transmitter which is believed to have had the capability, if perfected, of transmitting clear vocal speech across long distances. However, Reiss died prematurely, on January 14, 1874.

1865: **Antonio Meucci (USA)** receives patent for improved method of making wicks for candles, ones that burn without residue.

1865: **Antonio Meucci (USA)** receives patent for improved process for removing mineral, gummy, and resinous substances from vegetables, which enables the manufacture of high quality paper from wood and other vegetable fibers.

1866: **Benjamin Chew Tilghman (USA)** develops the sulfite pulping process, a chemical (rather than mechanical) process for making paper from wood pulp. The first mill to use this process will be built in Sweden in 1874.

1866: **Antonio Meucci (USA)** receives patent for his improvements to the process for making paper pulp from wood. He used a chemical process that could also be applied to hay, leaves, rope, and various other vegetable substances making them into paper.

1868: **Georges Leclanché (France)** invents the dry cell battery, which is very similar to the AAA-D cell batteries used today. *Antonio Meucci uses this battery technology in his telettrofono, for which he made an application for a patent in 1871.*

1871: **Antonio Meucci, (USA)** receives "caveat" from US Patent Office for his sound telegraph – the first electric telephone instrument. It operates by the conducting effect of continuous metallic conductors as the medium for sound, and increases the effect by electrically insulating both the conductor and the parties who are communicating. This caveat was renewed in 1872, and 1873.

1871: **Charles Darwin (England)** publishes *The Descent of Man and Selection in Relation to Sex*, which presents his theories on the evolution of human beings and on sexual selection.

1871: **Z. T. Gramme and Hippolyte Fontaine (Belgium)** become the first large-scale manufacturers of practical AC and DC generators.

1876: **Antonio Meucci (USA)** receives a patent for making improvement in hygrometers – making them more sensitive to changes in atmospheric humidity.

1876: **Alexander Graham Bell (USA)** receives a patent for the invention of the telephone.

1876: **Elisha Gray (USA)** receives a "caveat" for the invention of the telephone, the description of which was substantially the same as the one submitted by Alexander Graham Bell. Both men submitted their applications on the same day, February 14, 1876, within two hours of each other. Bell's application was submitted first.

1876: **Nikolaus August Otto (Germany)** constructs the first four-stroke gas engine, the most direct ancestor to today's automobile engines.

1877: **Thomas A. Edison (USA)** invents the phonograph.

1878: New Haven, Connecticut becomes the site of the first commercial telephone exchange.

1879: **Thomas A. Edison (USA)** invents the electric light bulb.

1880: **Louis Pasteur (France)** publishes his landmark *Germ Theory of Disease*, arguing that all contagious microscopic organisms that damage the victim at the cellular level and are spread from person to person cause diseases.

1880-1889: The laboratories of **Robert Koch (Germany)** and **Louis Pasteur (France)** work simultaneously to discover the bacteria responsible for major diseases. They isolate the causes of tuberculosis (1882, the first microorganism associated with a specific human disease), cholera and diphtheria and develop a vaccine against rabies.

1882: **Thomas A. Edison (USA)** develops and installs the world's first large central electric-power station, in New York City. It used direct current (DC) power.

1885: **Gottlieb Daimler (Germany)** invents a high-speed internal-combustion engine (patented in 1887). This marks an important step in the development of the automobile.

1887: **Nicola Tesla (Europe, USA)** receives a set of patents covering the generation, transmission, and use of alternating current (AC) electricity. George Westinghouse quickly buys Tesla's patents and struggles with Edison over whether AC or DC power will become the US standard. Westinghouse eventually triumphs.

1888: *George Eastman (USA)* perfects the Kodak camera, the first camera designed to use the roll file he had invented two years earlier.

1888: *Heinrich Hertz (Germany)* produces, detects and identifies what we now call radio waves – electromagnetic radiation that is invisible to the human eye.

1891: *Almon Brown Strowger (USA)* patents the first automated telephone switching exchange, using direct dial (rather than a human operator) to connect the two parties.

1892: *Rudolf Diesel (Germany)* patents the internal combustion engine later named after him. It uses oil rather than gasoline.

1895: *Wilhelm Konrad Roentgen (Germany)* discovers x-rays.

1895: *Guglielmo Marconi (Italy, England)* develops a wireless telegraph after reading Herz's 1892 publication. Called the radiotelegraph (later shortened to radio), it is able to transmit signals (Morse code) over a distance of 3 kilometers by means of a directional antenna. The sending and receiving devices do not need to be connected by wires.

1897: *Alexander Popov (Russia)* develops an antenna to transmit radio waves over a distance (5 kilometers, at first).

1897: *Joseph John Thomson (England)* discovers the electron.

1898: *Marie and Pierre Curie (France)* discover the radioactive elements polonium and radium.

1898: *Valdemar Poulsen (Denmark)* patents the first device to record sound magnetically.

1899-1901: *Gugliemo Marconi (Italy, England)* successfully uses his radiotelegraph to communicate across the English Channel from England to France.

1900: *Reginald Fessenden (Canada, USA)* is the first to transmit human speech over radio waves using a spark-gap transmitter. His voice is heard one mile away by his assistant.

1903: *Wilbur and Orville Wright (USA)* successfully keep their airplane in flight for 12 seconds.

1910: *Thomas A. Edison (USA)* develops the alkaline cell, or nickel-iron battery that is used primarily in heavy industry applications today.

Glossary

More about important people in this book:

Bell, Alexander Graham (1847–1922): was born on March 3, 1847 in Edinburgh, Scotland, and he later lived in Canada and the United States. His mother, who was deaf, was a musician and a painter of portraits. His father, who taught deaf people how to speak, invented "Visible Speech". This was a code that showed how the tongue, lips, and throat were positioned to make speech sounds. Interested in working with the deaf throughout his life, Alexander Graham introduced his father's system of Visible Speech into practice in the U.S. when he obtained a teaching position at the Boston School for the Deaf. He later advanced to become a professor at Boston University teaching elocution. After several years of association and work with Charles Watson on harmonic vibrations produced by a tuning fork, and several months of work at Western Union laboratories with a team of people working on the electro-harmonic telegraph, he applied for a patent for the telephone. On March 7, 1876, the U.S. Patent Office granted Bell a patent for a communication device for "transmitting vocal or other sounds telegraphically." However, on September 25, 2001, the United States Congress officially recognized Antonio Meucci as the inventor of the telephone, denying Bell's claim to its invention.

Brugnatelli, Luigi Valentino (1761-1818): Physician, physicist and chemist, Brugnatelli was a leading researcher on galvanic gold plating. He published his findings in 1802 in the *Journal de Chimie et de Physique* in Belgium and again in 1805 in the *Philosophical Magazine*. He was also responsible for promoting periodical scientific literature in Italy, which is how Antonio Meucci came into contact with his work.

Bunsen, Robert Wilhelm von (1811-1889): German physicist and chemist, von Bunsen taught chemistry and became famous for his studies on chemical decomposition produced by electricity. He made a major contribution to the design of scientific equipment for laboratories, the most well known of these being the electric battery which bears his name. It was the Bunsen battery, which Antonio Meucci used in his experiments in Havana that led to his invention of the telephone.

Buonarroti, Michelangelo (1475 – 1564): In the 16th Century, he was one of the most famous sculptors of the Italian Renaissance. He was a also a painter, architect and poet, but most well known for his marble sculptures which reflected his deep study of anatomy and a true appreciation for the beauty of the human form. As a youth he became a life-long protégé of the ruling Medici family in Florence, Italy where he came into contact with the circle of political and cultural personalities that gravitated around the court. Some of his most famous works can be seen in Rome, where he sculpted the famous Vatican Pietà and painted a fresco in the Sistine Chapel of the Vatican and in Florence, where he sculpted the marble statue of David (Galleria dell'Accademia).

Copernicus, Nicolaus: In 1543 Copernicus had had a revolutionary idea: the earth is not the center of the solar system; rather, it revolves around the sun. No one had paid much attention to Copernicus, but when Galileo began to speak and write about his findings many more people listened. The idea that the earth revolved around the sun went against the teachings of the church, which eventually forced Galileo to state publicly that his theory was wrong –but it was not, of course, and eventually the world knew his observations had been valid.

da Vinci, Leonardo (1452-1514): Leonardo da Vinci was a Florentine renaissance painter, architect, engineer, mathematician and philosopher. He was, in fact, the leading Florentine painter and sculptor of his day. Leonardo was born on April 15, 1452, in the small Tuscan town of Vinci, near Florence. He was the son of a wealthy Florentine notary and a peasant woman. In the mid-1460s the family settled in Florence, where Leonardo was given the best education that Florence, the intellectual and artistic center of Italy, could offer. He was one of the greatest masters of Italy's High Renaissance. He is best known today as a painter, and his innovations in that field continued to have a profound impact in the art world long after his death. Many of his scientific studies – which included subjects as diverse as anatomy, optics and hydraulics – are remarkable for the way they anticipated modern inventions. In both science and art Leonardo placed a high value of precise scientific observation. He wrote his observations, often in hard to decipher mirror script, in a series of notebooks that were not published in his lifetime. He studied the circulation of the blood, learned anatomy by dissecting corpses, made discoveries in meteorology and geology, calculated the effect of the moon on the tides and formulated valid theories about how continents are formed. He is given credit for inventing the hydrometer (an instrument to measure either the specific gravity or density of a liquid) and was among the first to study hydraulics (the mechanics of fluids) as a science. Some of his most famous paintings include The Last Supper, a mural in the refectory of the Monastery of Santa Maria delle Grazie, Milan. Leonardo painted several portraits, but the only one that survives is the famous Mona Lisa (1503-06, Louvre). His innovations in the field of painting influenced the course of Italian art for more than a century after his death, and his scientific studies—particularly in the fields of anatomy, optics, and hydraulics—anticipated many of the developments of modern science.

Don Miguel Tacon Y Rosique (1775 - 1855): The Tacon Theater in Havana was named for this governor of Cuba, who had served in the Spanish army before Cuba was liberated from its status as a colony of Spain. Tacon was famous for his building efforts within Havana, for improving the public services and hygiene, fighting environmental pollution, and for improving public order. He modernized Havana, repairing streets, introducing new lighting, and building the Tacon Theater. In the year 1834 he addressed problems with the public markets, tearing down those that had poor ventilation and replacing them with modern ones with big marble slabs on which to display produce, running water to keep counters and utensils clean, large roads for traffic and porticos, or covered walkways for patrons to use to stay out of the sun and rain. He upgraded the sewerage system throughout the city and hired Don Manuel Pastor to upgrade the water system as well. The Tacon government of Havana ended in April 1838 and was succeeded eventually by Leopoldo O'Donnell.

Galilei, Galileo (1564 - 1642): Galileo was an Italian mathematics teacher, astronomer and physicist, and one of the first true scientists. Galileo learned that a pendulum took the same time to make a long swing as it did to make a short one—the scientific principle underlying modern clocks and time-keeping in general. He showed that light objects fell as fast as heavy ones when pulled toward the earth (gravity). He built a telescope and became the first person to use this tool to study the moon and planets. What he saw made Galileo believe Copernicus' idea that the Earth was not the center of the universe. The Church punished him for his belief in this idea. Later, scientists like Isaac Newton built new knowledge on Galileo's discoveries.

Galvani, Luigi (1737-1798): The Italian biologist, anatomist and physician Luigi Galvani was one of the first to investigate the phenomenon of what came to be named "bioelectrogenesis". In a series of experiments started around 1780, Galvani, working at the University of Bologna, found that the electric current delivered by a Leyden jar or a rotating static electricity generator would cause the contraction of the muscles in the leg of a frog and many other animals, either by applying the charge to the muscle or to the nerve. Galvani's remarkable experiments helped to establish the basis for the biological study of neurophysiology and neurology. He established that nerves were not water pipes or channels, as previously thought, but electrical conductors. Information within the nervous system was carried by electricity generated directly by the organic tissue. As the result of the experimental demonstrations carried out by Luigi Galvani and his followers, the electrical nature of the nerve-muscle function was unveiled. However, a direct proof could only be made when scientists could be able to measure or to detect the natural electrical currents generated in the nervous and muscular cells. Galvani did not have the technology to measure these currents, because they were too small.

Garibaldi, Giuseppe (1807-1888): Born on July 4, 1807, Garibaldi spent his youth as a sailor on Mediterranean merchant ships. In 1833 he joined a movement called Young Italy, which aimed to free the Italian people from outside rule (largely by Austria and France) and unify the country as a self-governing republic. This remained his life-long dream. In 1834 he fled Italy to escape execution (for plotting to seize a warship), and spent twelve years in South America, where he developed his skills as a military leader. In 1848, Garibaldi returned to find Italy under siege both from within (by the Pope, who wanted to Rome to become a city owned by the papacy) and from outside (by the Austrians who were hoping to capture control of the northern Italian city of Venice). Garibaldi rejoined the Italian movement for freedom and unification (the *Risorgimento* [Ree-sor-gee-me-en-toe], Italian for "revival") and organized about 3000 volunteers, whom he led first in fights against the Austrian occupiers and then against the French in Rome. But the French were victorious, and Garibaldi and his 5000 followers had to retreat through Austrian-controlled territory. Many of his followers was killed or captured and Garibaldi soon disbanded them and fled Italy, pursued by the Austrians and in fear for his life. His wife died in the escape, and Garibaldi began a five-year exile. Garibaldi's first stop in this, his second exile, had been Tangier. His second stop was the Meucci's Staten Island home.

Ghiberti, Lorenzo (1378-1455): Italian designer, sculptor, goldsmith, architect and writer. He was Florentine and first came to prominence as winner of the 1401 competition for a set of bronze doors to the Florence Baptistry. They are considered by many art historians to mark the beginning of the Renaissance. Their popular name- Doors of Paradise- is based on a tradition that the young Michelangelo, greatly impressed by the doors, described them as worthy to be the Gates of Paradise. The main panels were prepared by the famed lost wax process. Each panel was carefully modeled in wax and covered with liquid plaster and a clay jacket. The panels were then baked until the wax flowed away, leaving a mold into which molten bronze was poured. The bronze panels were allowed to cool slowly for several days, to prevent cracking, and then the clay and plaster were removed. After cleaning, each panel was chased, or worked in fine detail with metal tools, a process that took years. Then followed the dangerous fire-gilding process- a gold-mercury amalgam was applied to each panel and the toxic mercury fumes driven off by heating, leaving gold surfaces on the panels. The completed doors were installed in 1452. For five centuries the doors stood, weathering wars and floods, until the late years of World War II.

Grand Duchy and Duchess of Tuscany (1824 – 1859): Leopold II and Maria Carolina of Saxony held these titles during the time Antonio Meucci lived there. During his rule these 35 years, liberal reforms took place within the monarchy, opening up Tuscany to take part in movement toward independence from the royal families and the control of Austria over the region. The movement was for unification of all the regions into one republic, today known as Italy.

Gray, Elisha (1835-1901): was one of the most successful inventors in American history, so much so that he made millions by his patents. At college he became fascinated by electricity, and in 1867 he received a patent for an improved telegraph relay. During the rest of his life he was granted patents on about 70 other inventions, including the telautograph (1888), an electrical device for reproducing writing at a distance. On Feb. 14, 1876, Gray filed with the U.S. Patent Office a caveat (an announcement of an invention he expected soon to patent) describing apparatus 'for transmitting vocal sounds telegraphically.' This patent was granted to Alexander Graham Bell. In 1872, Gray founded the Western Electric Manufacturing Company, parent firm of the present Western Electric Company. Two years later he retired to continue independent research and invention and to teach at Oberlin College.

Jacobi, Moritz Hermann von (1801-1874): German physicist and engineer Moritz Hermann Jacobi worked mainly in Russia. His works on galvanoplastics, electric motors, and wire telegraphy were of great applied significance. He experimented extensively with the power of an electromagnet in relation to the design of motors and generators, and discussed his efforts to construct the first full-scale practical motor in May 1834. He carried out a number of tests on the motor for instance measuring its output by determining the amount of zinc consumed by the battery. It was his work in electrotyping and electroplating that influenced Antonio Meucci. Electrotyping is electroforming process for making duplicate plates for relief, or letterpress, printing. Jacobi first announced the process 1838 while working in St. Petersburg, Russia. Thomas Spencer and C.J. Jordan of England and Joseph A. Adams of the United States produced similar results the following year. An electrotype, or electro, is made by electroplating a thin shell of copper or other metal onto a mold, usually wax, of the original cut or type form and then removing the mold and backing the shell with metal. More durable than type and cuts, electros are used instead of the original for long press runs, to avoid wear and damage to expensive type and halftones or linecuts. Electrotypes also can duplicate and replace linoleum cuts, woodcuts, and wood engravings.

Marty y Torrens, Don Francisco: He built the Gran Teatro do Tacon, which was inaugurated on April 15, 1838. Born in Barcelona he arrived in Cuba while still a youth. Working his way from being a butcher, he opened a shop in Cuba and began building a fortune. Some claimed that he built this fortune as a slave trader, importing Africans from Africa and slaves from the coasts of Merida and Belize.

O'Donnell, Leopoldo (1809 - 1867): Beginning his governorship of Havana on October 21, 1843, O'Donnell was one of the youngest generals of the Spanish army. His legacy was as one of the cruelest, most bloodthirsty and predatory governors of Cuba. This reputation was based at least in part on his execution of seventy-eight people that took place in a racial uprising and his imprisonment and torture of 900 others. O'Donnell was governor of Cuba for four and a half years, during which time he contracted with Antonio Meucci to perform electroplating of the swords, buckles and helmets of his soldiers (See Chapter Five).

Salvi, Lorenzo: Native of Bergamo, Italy, he is reputed to have been the greatest tenor of his time. He regularly sang at La Scala Opera Theater in Milan, Italy as well as other famous opera houses, from Paris to London to Moscow, and St. Petersburg in Russia. He enjoyed great popularity also in New York where he agreed to sing on stage with the famous Swedish opera performer, Jenny Lind. According to the impresario, he was the "pet of the New York ladies." Lorenzo Salvi died in Bologna in 1879 at the age of 69. His close friendship with Antonio and Esterre Meucci began in Florence, Italy and continued as he traveled with them to Cuba and New York.

Volta, Alessandro (1745-1827): Count Alessandro Volta was born in Como, Italy, into a noble family. He was a pioneer in the field of **electrochemistry,** the branch of science dealing with the inter-conversion of chemical and electrical energies. The first electric battery was called 'pile,' invented by Count Volta, who was also professor of experimental physics at the University of Pavia. The invention of the battery lifted Volta's fame to its pinnacle. He was called to France by Napoleon in 1801 for a kind of "command performance" of his experiments. He received many medals and decorations, including the Legion of Honor, and was even made a count and, in 1810, a senator of the kingdom of Lombardy. Volta received his greatest honor, however, at the hands of no ruler, but of his fellow scientists. The unit of electromotive force- the driving force that moves the electric current- is now called the "volt."

More about the terms used in this book:

Acoustics: The way sound carries or can be heard within an enclosed space such as an auditorium. Acoustics also refers to the study of the physical properties of sound.

Affidavit: The written or printed statement of facts made voluntarily under oath by a party.

Animal Electricity: The human body contains an electrical system. Nerve fibers carry tiny electrical signals to the brain when we see, hear, taste, touch or smell. These electrical signals can be measured in tiny amounts. They travel throughout the body, especially in the brain, muscles, and sense organs. Although Volta rejected Galvani's idea of animal electricity, it wasn't entirely wrong.

Battery: The battery Volta discovered used two different metals and a wet or moist solution to conduct electricity and produce a constant flow of electric charge. Since Volta's discovery, battery technology has made giant strides. One important modification of Volta's device was the portable battery, discovered by Gaston Plante in 1859.

Caveat: A caveat was, in Antonio's time, given for inventions that were believed to need more work before being patented. They nonetheless established the inventor's *claim to* the invention. When caveats were issued the Patent Office was supposed to note the subject matter of the caveat and place the file in a confidential archive. If within one year another inventor had filed an application on a similar process or device, the Patent Office was to notify the holder of the caveat, who then had three months to submit a formal application. Caveats lasted one year and were renewable. Caveats were much less costly than a full patent application and required a less detailed description of the invention. The Patent Office stopped issuing caveats early in the 1900s.

Deposition: The oral testimony of a witness recorded in writing for use in a court case.

Dewpoint: The temperature to which the air must be cooled at constant barometric pressure for water vapor to condense into water. When the dewpoint falls below freezing it is called the frost point.

Electricity: Electricity is a form of energy, which when produced typically flows through wires. The wire is made up of billions of tiny particles called atoms. Each atom is too small to be seen but contains even smaller parts (nucleus and electron). The electron orbits the nucleus, and electricity is created when the path of the electron is disrupted and made to move faster. Magnets are used to make the electrons move faster. Produced electricity travels in a circuit when in a conductor. That is, it only flows if it can get back to its starting point. Electromagnetic waves, on the other hand, radiate.

Electroplating: Electroplating was discovered by Moritz Jacobi in 1838. The electrode on which the metal is "plated" or deposited is put in the solution and connected to the negative pole of an electric cell or power source. Another electrode, also immersed in the solution, is connected to the positive pole of the same electric cell.

Electrical Current: The flow of electrons (part of the atom) through a conductor. It may also be used to mean the rate at which an electric charge flows.

Electrostatic generator: An electrostatic generator produces high voltage static electricity. This type of electricity does not move in a current.

Electrical resistance: is a measure of the degree to which an object opposes the passage of an electrical current.

Helix: A spiral form or structure; a three-dimensional curve that lies on a cylinder or cone, so that its angle to a plan is perpendicular to the axis is constant.

Hourglass: An instrument for measuring time, consisting of two glass chambers connected by a narrow neck and containing a quantity of sand, mercury, or another flowing substance that trickles from the upper chamber to the lower in a fixed amount of time, often one hour.

Lightning Electricity: The lightning charge occurs when storm clouds gather and the water and ice particles inside them bump together. The bumping causes static electricity to build up. Positive charges collect in the highest clouds and negative charges in the lower. When the buildup of the charge is too great, a flash of lightening is released.

Patent: an official document issued by the U.S. Patent Office granting an inventor sole rights, including the right to market an invention.

Sources

Chapter Two - The Fireworks Go "Off"

"*each of the three defendants directly took part in lighting the Rockets of the Funnels...*" Auditor Director of the Legal Proceedings of Florence, Report Dated May 16, 1825 cited in: Catania, Basilio. *Antonio Meucci: The Inventor and His Times* (SEAT Publications, Turin, Italy) 1994, page 37.

"something special is in store..." Auditor Director of the Legal Proceedings of Florence, Report Dated May 16, 1825 cited in: Catania, Basilio. *Antonio Meucci: The Inventor and His Times* (SEAT Publications, Turin, Italy) 1994, page 37.

"*The deeds on the whole reveal...*" Police Superintendent of S. Spirito, May 30, 1825, ibid. Catania. Page 39.

"*This Meucci who neglected to warn his fellow gatekeeper...*" Sir Knight Colmo, Auditor of the President, May 30, 1825, ibid. Catania, page 38

"*I therefore believe that his defendant deserves to be mortified by five days in prison...*" Sir Knight Colmo, Auditor of the President, May 30, 1825, ibid Catania, page 39.

"Meucci shall be sentenced to eight days in prison..." Buon Governo, S. Spirito Police Precinct, Sent June 4, 1824, ibid. Catania, Page 40.

"Memorandum To the Most Illustrious Sir Knight President…" from the S. Spirito Precinct, 9 June 1825 , ibid. Catania, Pages 42 and 43.

"…*accepting the petition forwarded by his father,…*" C. Callepi, Police Superintendent, Sent June 9, 1825, ibid. Catania. Page 40.

Chapter Five - Water, Buckles and Swords

"…*People got up early in Havana…*" Otto Eduard, Reiseerinnungen on Cuba Nord und Sudamurkaj, 1834 – 1841, Verlog der Nauchschen Buchhandlung, Berlin, 1843. ibid Catania. Page 234.

"…*I had familiarized myself with galvanoplastic electricity….*" Antonio Meucci's Deposition for New York Circuit Court Case - Globe Telephone Company, Meucci et. al versus American Bell Telephone Company 1885 – 1887, cited in Schiavo, Giovanni. *Antonio Meucci: Inventor of the Telephone* (The Vigo Press, New York) 1958, Pages 209-230.

"…*I provide myself with the best books* …" ibid. Antonio Meucci's deposition, reprinted in Schiavo. Pages 209 – 230.

Chapter Six – Electric Shock Treatment

"…*The number of people in the streets began to increase….*" Op. cit. Otto Eduard reprinted in Catania. Page 268.

"…*The idea came to me to apply electricity to sick persons….*" Antonio Meucci's Proofs for New York Circuit Court Case - Globe Telephone Company,

Meucci et. al versus American Bell Telephone Company 1885-1887 cited in Schiavo, Page 209.

"...In my laboratory where I kept an instrument..." ibid. Antonio Meucci Proofs cited in Schiavo, Page 215.

"...I ordered the sick person to repeat the operation...." Antonio Meucci's Deposition, Schiavo Page 210.

"...experimenting, I found that I didn't need a current so strong..." Antonio Meucci's Deposition, Answer No. 540.

Chapter Seven – 'telettrofono'

"...I took the instrument that I brought from Havana..." Antonio Meucci's Deposition, Answer 17.

Chapter Eight – Candles and Paper

"...Gentlemen, I regret that I must tell you..." Letter from Giuseppe Garabaldi to his recognition committee in New York regarding the August 10, 1850 planned reception. Reprinted in the New York Evening Post as cited in Nese, Mario and Nicotra, Francesco *Antonio Meucci* (Editrie) 1989.

"... A friend of mine, Antonio Meucci...." Giuseppe Garibaldi memoir published by Theodore Dwight *Life of General Garibaldi*, New York, 1861.

"...My dearest boss Meucci...." Ibid. memoir.

Chapter Nine – Explosion on the Staten Island Ferry

"…Good morning, fine day…" Affidavit of Maria Ciuci, dated September 23, 1885 for New York Circuit Court Case - Globe Telephone Company, Meucci et. al versus American Bell Telephone Company 1885-1887.

Chapter Ten – The Patent Business

"…I prepared a description and specifications of my inventions…." Antonio Meucci Affidavit, cited in Schiavo, Page 141.

"…Your telegraphing will have to be experimented with considerably before it will be ready for a patent." Stetson letter to Meucci, dated January 13, 1872 entered into evidence in the New York Circuit Court case of Globe vs. Bell.

"…It is true that he would come to make experiments…" Antonio Meucci Deposition, Answer 550 cited in Schiavo Page 145.

"…I told Mr. Grant that I had an invention…" Antonio Meucci Affidavit, cited in Schiavo Page 158.

"…About the year 1876…" Antonio Meucci, Deposition, December 15, 1885, Answer 396.

"…During the last five years of her life…" Angelo Grandi Affidavit, partner in Globe Telephone Company, cited in Schiavo Page 37.

"…I would like to see my rights as inventor recognized…." Antonio Meucci letter to daughter of Gari-

baldi in Museo del Risorgimanto in Milan, Italy. Italian text reprinted by Monti in *Un Inventori Amico Di Garibaldi*.

Bibliography

Caso, Adolph. *They Too Made America Great—Lives of Italian Americans.* Branden Books, Boston, 1978.

Catania, Basilio. *Antonio Meucci: The Inventor and His Times* (SEAT Publications, Turin, Italy) 1994.

De Nonno, Tony. *Antonio Meucci: The Father of the Telephone.* A fourteen minute film (De Nonno Productions Incorporated) 1991.

Encyclopedia Britannica, 1911 Edition.

Gardner, Robert. *Electricity and Magnetism* (Twenty-First Century Books) 1994.

National Italian American Foundation. *Italians in America: A Celebration* (Mockingbird Press and Portfolio Press) 2001.

Nese, Marco. Nicotra, Francesco. *Antonio Meucci 1808 – 1889.* (Editrice Publisher) 1989.

Newton, Roger. *Galileo's Pendulum* (Harvard University Press) 2004.

Schiavo, Giovanni. *Antonio Meucci: Inventor of the Telephone* (The Vigo Press, New York, Limited Edition Print with 60 Facsimiles) 1958.

Schiavo, Giovanni. *Four centuries of Italian American History* (Vigo Press).

Shulman, Seth. *The Telephone Gambit: Chasing Alexander Graham Bell's Secret* (W.W. Norton & Company) 2008.

Snedded, Robert The History of Electricity: Advances That Have Changed the World (Thomas Learning, New York) 1994.

Swezey, Kenneth M. Science Shows You How *The Encyclopedia Americana -- International Edition* Vol. 13. Danbury, Connecticut: Grolier Incorporated, 1995.

U.S. Patent Office, Two patents in particular were consulted for this book: Patent No. 22,739 Dated January 25 for Manufacture of Candles, 1859; Patent No. 183,062 Dated October 10, 1876 for Improvements in Hygrometers.

U.S, Supreme Court archives, Washington D.C. contains *Meucci's Deposition* from December 7, 1885, to January 13, 1886 and his second *Deposition* September 11, 1886; *Meucci's Memorandum Book*; *Meucci's Affidavit* of October 9, 1885; and *Meucci's Caveat*. Judge Wallace's decision is recorded in the *Federal Reporter*, Vol. 32,729 available in most legal libraries in the U.S.

Index